Copyright © 2012 Jo Franks

Table of Contents

Table of Contents iii
Preface vi

Chapter 1
A-M 1
   "Gold Room" Scones 1
   Almond Ginger Pear Scones 2
   Apple & Raisin Scones 3
   Apple 'n' Honey Scones 3
   Apple and Honey Scones 4
   Apple Cheddar Scones 5
   Apple Oat Bran Scones 6
   Apple Scones 7
   Apple-Ginger Scones 7
   Apricot White Chocolate Walnut Scones 8
   Bannock 9
   Berkeley Scones 10
   Blueberry Scones 12
   Breakfast Scones 13
   Buckwheat Granola Scones 14
   Buttermilk Scones 15
   Buttermilk Scones - Part 1 16
   Buttermilk Scones - Part 2 16
   Cape Breton Scones 18
   Cheese Scones 18
   Cheese Scones ** 19
   Cherry Apple Scones 20
   Chocolate-Strawberry Scone Cake 21
   Chocolate-Stuffed Peanut Butter Scones 22
   Citrus Scones With Lemon Curd, Country Cream And Berries 23
   Classic Baking-Powder Biscuits 25
   Cornmeal-Raisin Scones 26

Cranberry-Orange Scones 27
Cravings Scones 28
Crystallized Ginger Scones 29
Currant Scones 30
Double Chocolate Scones 30
Dried Cherry Scones 32
Dried Fruit Cream Scones 32
Dried Tart Cheery Scones 33
English Crumpets 34
English Scones 35
English Scones 36
English Scones 37
Five-Fruit Granola Scones 38
Gingerbread Scones 38
Girdle Scones 40
Griddle Scones 41
Hamburger Petal Pie 41
Herb Scones 42
Herb Scones 43
Jammer Cream Scones 44
Lemon And Lime Curd 45
Lemon Cream Scones 46
Lemon Curd #2 47
Lemon Eclair Filling 47
Lemon Pecan Scones 48
Lemon Scones 49
Low-Fat Date Scones 50
Moist Spiced Apple Scones 51

Chapter 2

N-Z 53
Oat Scones with Apple-Pear Butter 53
Oatmeal Apple Cranberry Scones 54
Old Fashioned Cream Scones 55
Old Fashioned Scones 56
Orange Scones with Raspberry Filling 56
Raisin Scones 57
Raisin Scones 58
Real Orange And Currant Scones 59
Rosemary And Ham Scones 60
Salmon Cakes Salad 61
Sausage Balls - 1 62
Savory Cheese Scones 63

Table of Contents

Scones 63
Scones 65
Scones 65
Scones 66
Scones 67
Scones 68
Scottish Rock Buns 69
Scottish Rock Buns 70
Soda Scones 71
Sour Cherry And Vanilla Cream Scones 72
Sourdough Buttermilk Biscuits And Scones 73
Strawberry-Pecan Scones 74
Swiss Scones 75
Tart Cherry-&-Vanilla Scones 76
Tea Scones 77
Teatime Scones 77
Yogurt Cheddar Scones 78

Index **80**

Preface

Notice of Rights

All rights reserved. No part of this book may be reproduced or transmitted in any form by any means, electronic, mechanical, photocopying, recording, or otherwise, without the prior written permission of the publisher.

Notice of Liability

The information in this book is distributed on an "As Is" basis without warranty. While every precaution has been taken in the preparation of the book, neither the author nor the publisher shall have any liability to any person or entity with respect to any loss or damage caused or alleged to be caused directly or indirectly by the instructions contained in this book or by the products described in it.

Trademarks

Many of the designations used by manufacturers and sellers to distinguish their products are claimed as trademarks. Where those designations appear in this book, and the publisher was aware of a trademark claim, the designations appear as requested by the owner of the trademark. All other product names and services identified throughout this book are used in editorial fashion only and for the benefit of such companies with no intention of infringement of the trademark. No such use, or the use of any trade name, is intended to convey endorsement or other affiliation with this book.

Jo Franks

Chapter 1
A–M

"GOLD ROOM" SCONES

20 servings
Source: Scone Greats

3 ⅔ cups **Flour**	2 **Eggs**
½ cup **Sugar**	¾ cups **Whole milk**
1 ½ tablespoons **Baking powder**	¾ cups **Raisins**
1 teaspoon **Salt**	⅓ cup **Honey**
½ cup **Butter**	

Preheat the oven to 425°F. Combine the flour, sugar, baking powder, and salt in a large bowl. Mix well. Cut the butter into the flour mixture with a pastry blender until the mixture resembles coarse cornmeal. Add the eggs, milk and raisins.

Stir quickly with a fork until the dough leaves the sides of the bowl and forms a ball. Spoon onto an ungreased cookie sheet to form the desired number of scones. Leave at least 1" between the scones. Bake until golden (about 12–15 minutes). Remove to a wire rack, and brush immediately with honey. Serve at once with butter, jam and whipped cream.

ALMOND GINGER PEAR SCONES

12 servings
Source: Scone Greats

2 cups **all-purpose flour**

1 cup **sugar**

1 teaspoon **baking powder**

1 teaspoon **ground ginger**

½ teaspoon **baking soda**

½ teaspoon **salt**

½ cup **butter, cut into 8 or 10 chunks**

¾ cups **diced dried pears**

½ cup **slivered almonds, toasted, divided**

⅓ cup **chopped candied ginger**

⅔ cups **buttermilk**

1 **egg, beaten, for glaze**

Additional sugar, for glaze

Heat oven to 425°F.

In large bowl mix flour, sugar, baking powder, ground ginger, baking soda and salt. Cut in butter with pastry blender or two knives until mixture resembles coarse crumbs. Add the pears, 1/3 cup of the almonds and the candied ginger; toss. Mix in buttermilk just to blend.

Gather into a ball and gently knead 3 or 4 times on lightly floured surface. or roll out 3/4-inch thick. Cut out circles with 2 1/2- to 3-inch round cutter, rerolling scraps as needed.

Place on baking sheet, spacing apart. Brush tops with egg, sprinkle with remaining almonds, dividing equally, and sprinkle with sugar.

Bake in center of oven 12 to 15 minutes until springy to the touch and lightly browned. Remove to rack to cool. Serve warm or at room temperature.

Chapter 1: A–M

APPLE & RAISIN SCONES

8 servings
Source: Scone Greats

½ cup **Dried apples**
1 ½ cups **Wheat germ original or honey crunch**
½ cup **Whole wheat flour**
1 tablespoon **Baking powder**
⅓ cup **Margarine**
½ cup **Raisins**
⅓ cup **Lowfat 2% milk**
2 **Egg whites, slightly beaten**

Preheat oven to 400°F.

Coarsely chop the apples; set aside. Combine the wheat germ, flour, sugar, and baking powder. Cut in the margarine until the mixture resembles coarse crumbs. Stir in the raisins and apples.

Combine the milk and egg whites; add to the dry ingredients, mixing just until moistened. Turn the dough out onto an ungreased cookie sheet; into a 9-inch circle.

Cut into eight wedges; do not separate.

Bake for 12 to 15 minutes, or until light golden brown. Break apart; serve warm with margarine, fruit spread or honey, if desired.

APPLE 'N' HONEY SCONES

10 servings
Source: Scone Greats

2 cups **All purpose flour**
⅔ cups **Wheat germ**
2 teaspoons **Baking powder**
1 teaspoon **Ground cinnamon**
¼ teaspoon **Ground nutmeg**
¼ teaspoon **Baking soda**
¼ teaspoon **Salt, optional**
⅓ cup **Margarine, chilled**
1 ¼ cups **Apples, finely chopped**

Scone Greats

(1 large apple)
½ cup **Skim milk**
¼ cup **Honey**
---TOPPING---

1 tablespoon **Wheat germ**
1 tablespoon **Sugar**
¼ teaspoon **Ground cinnamon**

Heat oven 400°F. Lightly spray large cookie sheet with nonstick cooking spray or grease lightly. Handle the dough gently. Over mixing scones can make them tough. Combine flour, wheat germ, baking powder, spices, baking soda and salt (if using). Cut in margarine until mixture resembles coarse crumbs.

Add combined apple, milk and honey, mixing just until dry ingredients are moistened. Turn dough out onto lightly floured surface; knead gently 5 to 6 times. dough into 9-inch circle. Mix together topping ingredients.

Sprinkle over dough. Cut dough into 10 wedges. Place 1/2-inch apart on prepared cookie sheet. Bake 16 to 18 minutes or until light golden brown.

APPLE AND HONEY SCONES

8 servings
Source: Scone Greats

2 cups **All-purpose flour**
⅔ cups **Wheat germ**
2 teaspoons **Baking powder**
1 teaspoon **Ground cinnamon**
¼ teaspoon **Baking soda**
¼ teaspoon **Salt**
¼ teaspoon **Ground nutmeg**

⅓ cup **Butter or margarine, cold**
1 lg **Tart apples, peeled and chop ped**
½ cup **Milk**
¼ cup **Honey**
Topping
2 teaspoons **Wheat germ**
2 teaspoons **Sugar**

Chapter 1: A–M

¼ teaspoon **Ground cinnamon**

In a large bowl, combine flour, wheat germ, baking powder, cinnamon, baking soda, salt and nutmeg. Cut in the butter until the mixture resembles coarse crumbs. combine the apple, milk and honey; add to dry ingredients just until moistened. Turn onto a floured surface, knead gently 5-6 times.

Gently pat dough into a 9-in. circle, 1/2 in. thick. Combine topping ingredients; sprinkle over dough. Cut into eight wedges and place on a greased baking sheet. Bake at 400°F for 15-18 minutes.

APPLE CHEDDAR SCONES

6 servings
Source: Scone Greats

1 ½ cups **All-purpose flour**

½ cup **Toasted wheat germ**

3 tablespoons **Granulated sugar**

2 teaspoons **Baking powder**

½ teaspoon **Salt**

2 tablespoons **Butter**

1 sm **Rome apple, chopped**

¼ cup **Shredded cheddar cheese**

1 lg **Egg white**

½ cup **Lowfat 1% milk**

Preheat oven to 400 degrees; grease an 8-inch round cake pan. In a medium bowl, combine the flour, wheat germ, sugar, baking powder and salt. With 2 knives or a pastry blender, cut in the butter until the size of coarse crumbs. Toss the chopped apple and cheese in the flour mixture.

Beat together the egg white and milk until well combined. Add to the flour mixture, mixing with a fork until a dough forms. Turn the dough out onto a lightly floured surface and knead 6 times.

Spread the dough evenly in the cake pan and score deeply with a knife into 6 wedges. Bake for 25 to 30 minutes, or until the top springs back when gently pressed. Let stand for 5 minutes; remove from the pan. Cool before serving.

APPLE OAT BRAN SCONES

8 servings
Source: Scone Greats

- 3 cups **All-purpose flour**
- 1 cup **Bran flakes cereal, oat or wheat**
- 4 teaspoons **Baking powder**
- 1 teaspoon **Ground cinnamon**
- ½ teaspoon **Salt**
- ¾ cups **Milk**
- ¼ cup **Vegetable oil**
- ¼ cup **Light brown sugar, packed**
- 1 lg **Egg**
- 1 lg **Red apple, cored unpeeled and coarsely chop**
- 1 tablespoon **Butter, melted**
- **Ground cinnamon, optional**

Preheat oven to 425 °F.

Grease a large baking sheet. In a large bowl, combine flour, cereal, baking powder, cinnamon and salt.

In a medium bowl, beat together milk, oil, sugar and egg. Add to dry ingredients along with chopped apple; mix lightly with a fork until mixture clings together and forms a soft dough.

Turn dough out onto a lightly floured surface and knead gently 5 or 6 times.

Divide dough in half. With a lightly floured rolling pin, roll one half of the dough into a 7-inch round; cut into 4 wedges.

Chapter 1: A–M

Repeat with remaining dough.

Place scones one inch apart on prepared pan. Pierce tops with the tines of a fork.

Brush tops with melted butter and sprinkle with additional cinnamon, if desired.

Bake for 15 to 18 minutes, or until golden brown. Serve warm.

APPLE SCONES

18 servings
Source: Scone Greats

2 cups **Flour**

3 teaspoons **Baking Powder**

2 tablespoons **Sugar**

½ teaspoon **Cinnamon**

½ teaspoon **Salt**

6 tablespoons **Shortening**

½ cup **Apples, peeled, chopped fine**

½ cup **Raisins**

4 tablespoons **Cold Apple juice or water**

Preheat oven to 400°F Mix together dry ingredients. Cut in shortening as you would for a pie crust. Stir in apples and raisins. Add enough juice to make a stiff dough.

On floured surface, roll dough about 1/2" thick. Cut into triangles and bake on cookie sheet for 10 minutes, or until light brown.

APPLE-GINGER SCONES

8 servings
Source: Scone Greats

Scone Greats

2 cups **Bisquick**

½ cup **Apple; chopped, peeled**

3 tablespoons **Brown sugar**

¼ teaspoon **Ginger**

⅓ cup **Milk**

1 **Egg, or 2 egg whites or 1/4 c egg substitute**

Milk

Sugar

Heat oven to 425°F. Grease cookie sheet. Mix bisquick, apple, brown sugar, ginger, milk and egg until dough forms. Knead 10 times.

dough into 8 inch wide circle on cookie sheet. Brush with milk. Sprinkle with sugar. Cut into 8 wedges.

Bake about 14 minutes or untl golden brown. Serve warm.

APRICOT WHITE CHOCOLATE WALNUT SCONES

8 servings
Source: Scone Greats

2 cups **All-purpose flour**

⅓ cup **Granulated sugar**

2 teaspoons **Baking powder**

½ teaspoon **Salt**

¼ cup **Unsalted butter, chilled**

½ cup **Heavy (whipping) cream**

1 lg **Egg**

1 ½ teaspoons **Vanilla extract**

6 ounces **White chocolate, cut into 1/2 inch chunks***

1 cup **Toasted coarsely broken walnuts****

1 cup **Finely chopped dried apricots**

Preheat oven to 375°F. In a large bowl, stir together the flour, sugar, baking powder, and salt. Cut the butter into 1/2 inch cubes and distribute them over the flour mixture. With a pastry blender or two knives used scissors fashion, cut in the butter until the mixture resembles coarse crumbs. In a small bowl, stir together the cream, egg, and vanilla. Add the cream mixture to the flour mixture and knead until combined. Knead in the white chocolate, walnuts, and apricots.

With lightly floured hands, the dough out on a floured work surface to a thickness of 5/8 inch. Cut circles in the dough with a biscuit cutter. Gather the scraps of dough together and repeat till all the dough is used. Bake scones on ungreased baking sheet for 15 to 20 minutes, or until lightly browned on top. Place baking sheet on wire rack for 5 minutes, then transfer scones to wire rack to cool. Serve warm or cool completely and store in an airtight container. Makes 8 or 9 scones.

* (speaking) You can use those "Nestles Treasures" white chocolate chips, but before they came out with those, I used to use a Nestle Alpine White With Almonds bar, smashed into pieces. I would then omit the walnuts and substitute half the vanilla extract with almond extract for a delicious variation.

** To toast walnuts, place the walnuts in a single layer on a baking sheet and bake at 375°F for 5 to 7 minutes, shaking the sheet a couple of times, until the nuts are fragrant.

BANNOCK

6 servings
Source: Scone Greats

1 cup **Whole wheat flour**

½ cup **All purpose flour**

½ cup **Rolled oats**

2 tablespoons **Sugar, granulated**

2 teaspoons **Baking powder**

½ teaspoon –**Salt**

2 tablespoons **Butter, melted**

⅓ cup **Raisins, optional**

¾ cups –**Water, approx,**

Scone Greats

Bannock, a simple type of scone was cooked in pioneer days over open fires. Variations in flours and the additional of dried or fresh fruit make this bread the simple choice of Canadian campers even today.

Oven baking has become an acceptable alternative to the cast iron fry pan. For plain bannock, omit rolled oats and increase the all purpose flour to 1 cup. One of the earliest quick breads, bannock was as simple as flour, salt, a bit of fat (often bacon grease) and water. In gold rush days, dough was mixed right in the prospector's flour bag and cooked in a fry pan over an open fire. Indians wrapped a similar dough around sticks driven into the ground beside their camp fire, baking it along with freshly caught fish.

Stir together flours, oats, sugar, baking powder and salt. Add melted butter, raisins (if using) and water, adding more water if needed to make sticky dough. With floured hands, into greased pie plate.

Bake in 400°F oven for 20 to 25 minutes or until browned and tester comes out clean.

Cut into wedges.

SERVES:6

VARIATIONS: In place of raisins add chopped dried apricots or fresh berries.(Blueberries are terrific if one is camping in northern Ontario in .)

BERKELEY SCONES

1 servings
Source: Scone Greats

2 cups **unbleached all-purpose flour**

½ teaspoon **baking soda**

1 tablespoon **baking powder**

½ teaspoon **kosher salt**

Chapter 1: A–M

⅔ cup **plus 2 tablespoons sugar, divided**

1 ½ cups **medium-grind yellow cornmeal**

1 cup **cold, (2 sticks) unsalted butter, cut into 1-inch cubes**

¾ cup **dried sweet cherries**

1 cup **buttermilk**

1. Heat the oven to 425 degrees. Line 2 baking sheets with parchment paper.

2. Sift the flour, baking soda and baking powder together into a large bowl. Add the salt, two-thirds cup sugar, and the cornmeal to the bowl and stir with a wooden spoon until combined.

3. Add the butter and cut in with a pastry cutter or 2 dinner knives, until it is the size of small peas. Using the spoon, mix in the cherries. Make a well in the center and add the buttermilk. Mix briefly, just until the ingredients come together; some loose flour should remain at the bottom of the bowl. The dough will be stiff and slightly sticky. Let the batter stand for 5 minutes.

4. Gently shape the dough into balls about 2 1/4 inches in diameter and place them on the prepared pans about 2 inches apart.

5. Sprinkle the remaining sugar on top of the scones. Place the scones on the middle rack and immediately turn the oven temperature down to 375 degrees. Bake for 20 to 25 minutes, or until the scones are golden. Transfer the scones to a wire rack and cool.

Each scone: 297 calories; 4 grams protein; 40 grams carbohydrates; 2 grams fiber; 14 grams fat; 8 grams saturated fat; 36 mg. cholesterol; 224 mg. sodium.

Servings: 14 (makes 14 scones)

Scone Greats

BLUEBERRY SCONES

8 servings
Source: Scone Greats

2 cups **all-purpose flour**

3 tablespoons **sugar, plus more**

1 tablespoon **baking powder**

¾ teaspoon **salt**

6 tablespoons **cold unsalted butter, cut into pieces**

1 ½ cups **rinsed fresh blueberries, picked over**

1 teaspoon **grated lemon zest**

⅓ cup **heavy cream, plus more**

2 **large eggs, lightly beaten**

Adjust rack to center of oven, and heat to 400 degrees.

Place a Silp at baking mat on a baking sheet, and set aside.

In a large bowl, sift together flour, 3 tablespoons sugar, baking powder, and salt.

Using a pastry blender, or two knives, cut in butter until the largest pieces are the size of small peas.

Stir in blueberries and zest.

Using a fork, whisk together cream and egg in a liquid measuring cup.

Make a well in the center of dry ingredients and pour in cream mixture.

Stir lightly with fork just until dough comes together.

Turn out onto a lightly floured surface, and knead a few times to mix well.

Pat dough into a 6-inch square about 1 1/4 inches thick.

Using a floured knife, cut into four 3-inch squares.

Cut squares in half on the diagonal to form eight triangles.

Transfer to prepared baking sheet.

Brush tops with cream and sprinkle with sugar.

Bake until golden brown, 20 to 22 minutes.

Transfer scones from baking sheet to wire racks to cool.

Makes 8.

BREAKFAST SCONES

16 servings
Source: Scone Greats

- 1 ½ cups **Whole wheat pastry flour**
- ⅓ cup **Wholemeal flour**
- ¾ cups **Wheat bran**
- 1 teaspoon **Baking powder**
- 2 tablespoons **Soy margarine**
- 2 tablespoons **Corn syrup**
- 1 cup **Potato or soy milk**

Mix dry ingredients. Add margarine and mix well. Add the syrup and enough milk to make a loose dough.

Turn onto a floured board and knead until smooth. Roll out into a square with a thickness of about 1/4 inch. Cut dough in half, then into quarters and then to eights.

Bake on a lightly floured baking sheet at 400°F for approximately 20 minutes. Cool on a wire rack. Split and serve with whole fruit preserves.

Total calories per serving-79 Fat-2grams

BUCKWHEAT GRANOLA SCONES

8 servings
Source: Scone Greats

1 ⅓ cups **All-purpose flour**

⅔ cups **Buckwheat flour**

¼ cup **Brown sugar, packed**

2 ¼ teaspoons **Baking powder**

⅓ cup **Butter, chilled; cut up**

⅓ cup **Milk**

1 lg **Egg**

1 teaspoon **Vanilla extract, or maple extract**

1 ½ cups **Granola, homemade preferred**

Preheat oven to 375°F; lightly butter a cookie sheet. In a large bowl, stir together the flours, brown sugar and baking powder.

Add the butter. Using a pastry cutter, cut in the butter until the mixture is the texture of cornmeal.

In a separate bowl, mix the milk, egg and vanilla extract. Stir into the flour mixture.

The dough will be sticky. With lightly floured hands, knead in the granola.

Use an ice cream scoop or 1/3 cup measure to spoon the dough onto the cookie sheet, spacing them 2 1/2 to 3 inches apart.

Bake for 20 to 25 minutes, or until a toothpick inserted in the center comes out clean.

Remove from the oven and place on wire racks.

Serve warm or cold.

BUTTERMILK SCONES

18 servings
Source: Scone Greats

3 cups **Flour**
⅓ cup **Sugar**
2 ½ teaspoons **Baking powder**
½ teaspoon **Baking soda**
¾ teaspoons **Salt**
12 tablespoons **Butter**

1 cup **Buttermilk**
¾ cups **Currants**
1 teaspoon **Grated orange rind (orange part, or zest only)**

----GLAZE---- tb Heavy cream 1/4 ts Cinnamon tb Sugar

PREHEAT THE OVEN TO 425°F. Use an ungreased baking sheet. Combine the flour, sugar, baking powder, baking soda and salt in a mixing bowl. Stir well with a fork to mix and aerate. Add the butter and cut into the flour mixture, using a pastry blender or two knives, or work in, using your fingertips, until the mixture looks like fresh bread crumbs. Add the buttermilk, currants and orange rind. Mix only until the dry ingredients are moistened. Gather the dough into a ball and press so it holds together. Turn the dough out onto a lightly floured surface. Knead lightly 12 times. the dough into a circle 1/2-inch thick.

TO MAKE THE GLAZE: In a small bowl combine the cream, cinnamon and sugar; stir to blend. Brush the dough with the glaze. Cut the dough into 18 pie-shaped pieces. Place the scones 1 inch apart on the baking sheet. Bake for about 12 minutes or until the tops are browned. Serve hot.

BUTTERMILK SCONES - PART 1

12 servings
Source: Scone Greats

--For the scones:---

3 cups **All-purpose flour**

⅓ cup **Sugar**

2 ½ teaspoons **Baking powder**

½ teaspoon **Baking soda**

¾ teaspoons **Salt**

1 ½ **Cold unsalted butter**

(6 ozs) cut in small pieces

1 cup **Buttermilk,** (approximately)

1 tablespoon **Grated orange or lemon zest**

--For the topping:---

½ **Unsalted butter**

(2 ozs) melted,

For brushing

¼ cup **Sugar, for dusting -** Filling for rolled scones:

4 tablespoons **Jam or jelly, and/or**

4 tablespoons **Diced or small plump dried**

--fruits:---

(optional)

Currants/ raisins/ a pricots/ figs

The - See Part 2.

BUTTERMILK SCONES - PART 2

12 servings
Source: Scone Greats

See below

The - Position the oven racks to divide the oven into thirds and preheat the oven to 425°F. For the scones: In a medium bowl, stir the flour, sugar, baking powder, baking soda and salt together with a

Chapter 1: A-M

fork. Add the cold butter pieces and, using your fingertips (the first choice), a pastry blender or two knives, work the butter into the dry ingredients until the mixture resembles coarse cornmeal.

It's okay if some largish pieces of butter remain -- they'll add to the scones' flakiness. Pour in 1 cup buttermilk, toss in the zest, and mix with the fork only until the ingredients are just moistened -- you'll have a soft dough with a rough look. (If the dough looks dry, add another tablespoon of buttermilk.) Gather the dough into a ball, pressing it gently so that it holds together, turn it out onto a lightly floured work surface, and knead it very briefly ~- a dozen turns should do it. Cut the dough in half. For triangular-shaped scones: Roll one half of the dough into a /2-inch-thick circle that is about 7 inches across. Brush with half of the melted butter for the topping, sprinkle with 2 tablespoons of the sugar, and cut the circle into 6 triangles.

Place the scones on an ungreased baking sheet and set aside while you roll out the other half. For the rolled scones: Roll one half of dough into a strip 12 inches long and 1/2 inch thick (the piece will not be very wide). Spread the strip with half of the melted butter for the topping and dust with half of the sugar. If you want to spread the roll with jam and/or sprinkle it with dried fruits, now's the time to do so; leave a narrow border along one long edge bare. Roll the strip up from the other long side like a jelly roll; pinch the seam closed and turn the roll seam-side down.

Cut the roll in half and cut each piece into six 1-inch-wide roll-ups. Place the rolled scones cut-side down on an ungreased baking sheet, leaving a little space between each one. Repeat with the remaining dough. Bake the scones in the preheated oven for 10 to 12 minutes, until both the tops and bottoms are golden. Transfer the scones to a rack to cool slightly. These are best served warm but are just fine at room temperature. If you're not going to eat the scones the same day, wrap them airtight and freeze; they'll stay fresh for a month. To serve, defrost the scones at room temperature in their wrappers, then

Scone Greats

unwrap and reheat on a baking sheet for 5 minutes in a 350°F oven. 12 Triangular or 24 rolled scones.

CAPE BRETON SCONES

1 servings
Source: Scone Greats

2 cups **Flour**

2 tablespoons **Sugar**

1 tablespoon **Baking powder**

1 teaspoon **-salt**

¼ teaspoon **Basking soda**

1 cup **Raisins or currants**

½ cup **Sour cream**

¼ cup **Oil**

3 tablespoons **Milk**

Egg;slightly beaten Sift together dry ingredients and stir in the raisins. Blend the remaining ingredients and stir in the flour mixture until the dough is all together.

Toss on a lightly floured surface until no longer sticky. Knead a few times. Divide the dough in half then each ball of dough into a 6 " circle with the top slightly rounded. Brush the tops with milk and sprinkle with sugar. Cut each circle into 6 wedges.

Place 2 inches apart on a cookie sheet. Bake at 425°F for 10 to 12 minutes or till golden. Serve hot with butter and jam or flavoured butter or honey.

CHEESE SCONES

12 servings
Source: Scone Greats

1 cup **All-purpose flour**

1 ½ teaspoons **Baking powder**

1 teaspoon **Dry mustard**

pn **Salt**

Chapter 1: A-M

1 cup **Whole-wheat flour**

3 teaspoons **Cold butter or margarine, cut in small pieces**

¾ cups **(3oz) finely shredded sharp Cheddar cheese**

⅔ cups **Milk (about)**

Butter

This qualifies as a savory; a bit of a change from the usual scone.

Preheat oven to 425°F (220°C). Lightly grease a large baking sheet; set aside. Sift all-purpose flour, baking powder, dry mustard and salt into a large bowl. Stir in the whole-wheat flour. With your fingers, rub in cold butter until mixture is crumbly. Stir in 1/2 cup cheese. Make a well in center of mixture; add milk and mix with a fork to make a dough that BARELY holds together (you need to press dough together with your hands).

Turn out onto floured surface and knead lightly. Roll out with a floured rolling pin or dough with your hands to make a round about 3/4-inch thick. Cut into rounds with a 2-inch fluted or plain cookie cutter. Place to 1 1/2 inches apart on baking sheet; sprinkle with remaining 1/4 cup cheese. Bake 8-10 minutes or until well risen and golden. Transfer to a wire rack to cool. When cold, split and serve with butter. Makes about 12 scones.

CHEESE SCONES **

8 servings
Source: Scone Greats

2 cups **All-Purpose Flour**

¾ cups **Grated Parmesan Cheese**

2 teaspoons **Baking Powder**

1 teaspoon **Dried Oregano, Crumbled**

¼ teaspoon **Salt**

4 tablespoons **Butter, Chilled And Cut Into Small Pieces**

½ cup **Milk**

2 lg **Eggs, Lightly Beaten**

1 teaspoon **Tabasco Pepper Sauce**

¾ cups **Finely Chopped Onion**

Hot from the oven, these scones are really good eating, especially with vegetable soup. To vary the flavor, throw in a half cup of chopped reconstituted sun-dried tomatoes, make them with Cheddar cheese instead of Parmesan, or try other herbs such as basil or dill. Preheat the oven to 400°F In a large bowl or a food processor, mix the flour, cheese, baking powder, oregano and salt. Cut in the butter, using a pastry blender, two knives, or pulses of the food processor, until the mixture resembles coarse crumbs. Transfer the mixture to a large bowl, if blended in a food processor.

In a small bowl, stir together the milk, eggs and Tabasco sauce. Make a well in the center of the dry ingredients and add the milk mixture, stirring to combine. Mix in the onion. The dough will be sticky.

Lightly butter a baking sheet. With lightly floured hands, the dough into a 9 inch circle in the center of the baking sheet. Cut the circle into 8 wedges. Bake the scones for 20 to 25 minutes, or until lightly browned.

CHERRY APPLE SCONES

12 servings
Source: Scone Greats

- 1 ½ cups **All-purpose flour, unbleache**
- ¾ cups **Whole wheat flour**
- 3 tablespoons **Granulated sugar**
- 2 teaspoons **Baking powder**
- ½ teaspoon **Baking soda**
- 1 **Egg white**
- ¾ cups **Unsweetened applesauce, plus**
- 2 tablespoons **Unsweetened applesauce**
- ⅓ cup **Dried cherries**
- **Skim milk or 1 beaten egg white**

Preheat oven to 375 degrees; coat a baking sheet with nonstick cooking spray. Combine the flours, sugar, baking powder and baking soda; stir to mix well. Stir in the egg white and just enough of the applesauce to form a stiff dough. Stir in the dried cherries. Form the dough into a ball and turn onto a lightly floured surface. With floured hands, the dough into a 7-inch circle.

Place the dough on the baking sheet and use a sharp floured knife to cut it into 12 wedges. Pull the wedges out slightly to leave a 1/2-inch space between them. Brush the tops lightly with skim milk or beaten egg white. Bake for about 20 minutes, or until lightly browned. Transfer to a serving plate and serve hot with cherry fruit spread or apple jelly.

Nutrition Analysis: 118 calories, 3.1g protein, 0.3g fat, 0mg cholesterol, mg sodium.

CHOCOLATE-STRAWBERRY SCONE CAKE

1 servings
Source: Scone Greats

2 ½ cups **Flour**

¼ cup **Sugar**

4 teaspoons **Baking powder**

¼ teaspoon **Salt**

⅔ cups **Butter or margarine; room temp.**

⅔ cups **Milk**

2 **Eggs**

1 package **Semisweet chocolate chips (6 oz)**

1 cup **Whipping cream**

2 **Baskets strawberries Stemmed and sliced**

In a bowl, combine flour, sugar, baking powder and salt. Cut in butter until mixture resembles coarse meal. In a small bowl, combine milk, 1 whole egg and 1 egg yolk. Mix into dry ingredients JUST until moistened.

Turn out onto lightly floured board; knead lightly several times, then bring dough together to form a ball. Divide in half; each half into a circle 8-inches in diameter. Place one circle on greased baking sheet; cover evenly with chocolate chips. Top with remaining circle; pressing lightly to seal edges. Beat remaining egg white.

Brush top of scone cake with egg white. Sprinkle generously with additional sugar. With a sharp knife, slice halfway through top layer to form six wedges. Bake in a preheated 425` oven for 18 to 20 minutes, until golden and springy to the touch. Transfer to a rack to cool slightly. Whip cream, add 1 cup of the berries. Sweeten to taste. Serve wedges of warm scone cake with remaining berries and strawberry whipped cream.

CHOCOLATE-STUFFED PEANUT BUTTER SCONES

16 servings
Source: Scone Greats

2 cups **flour**

½ cup **sugar, brown, light**

2 ½ teaspoons **baking powder**

¼ teaspoon **salt**

¼ cup **butter, sweet, chilled**

¾ cups **peanut butter, creamy**

¼ cup **milk**

2 **egg**

2 teaspoons **vanilla extract**

½ cup **peanuts, unsalted, chopped**

1 ½ ounces **chocolate, bittersweet, broken**

Preheat oven to 375°F. In a large bowl, stir together the flour, brown sugar, baking powder, and salt. Cut the butter into 1/2-inch cubes and distribute them over the flour mixture.

With a pastry blender or two knives used scissors fashion, cut in the butter until the mixture resembles coarse crumbs. In a small bowl, stir together the peanut butter, milk, eggs, and vanilla. Add the peanut butter mixture to the flour mixture and knead until combined. Knead in the peanuts. Pat the dough out into a 1/2-inch thickness on a cutting board.

Using a floured 2-1/2-inch to 3-inch diameter crinkled round biscuit cutter, cut out rounds from the dough. Gather the scraps together and repeat until all the dough is used and there are 16 rounds. Place 8 of the rounds on an ungreased baking sheet.

Top each round with a piece of the chocolate and one of the remaining circles of dough. Press the edges gently to seal. Bake for 17 to 19 minutes, or until lightly browned. Remove the baking sheet to a wire rack and cool for 5 minutes.

Using a spatula, transfer the scones to the wire rack to cool. Serve warm or cool completely and store in an airtight container. Yield: 8 scones.

VARIATION: Make the dough as above, omitting bittersweet chocolate, substituting 1/2 cup unsalted whole peanuts for the chopped peanuts and kneading in 3/4 cup of semisweet chocolate chips at the same time. Pat the dough into a 9-inch diameter circle on a baking sheet.

With a serrated knife, cut into 8 wedges. Bake for 20 to 22 minutes, or until a cake tester or toothpick inserted into the center of a scone comes out clean. Cool as above and recut into wedges, if necessary.

CITRUS SCONES WITH LEMON CURD, COUNTRY CREAM AND BERRIES

6 servings
Source: Scone Greats

2 ¼ cups **all-purpose flour**

¼ cup **sugar**

¾ teaspoons **baking soda**

1 teaspoon **baking powder**

Scone Greats

½ teaspoon **salt**

¼ teaspoon **nutmeg**

8 tablespoons **butter**

2 tablespoons **lemon zest, finely minced**

2 tablespoons **orange zest, finely minced**

1 large **egg, separated**

¾ cups **buttermilk**

extra **sugar, for sprinkling**

*****LEMON CURD*****

2 **eggs**

2 **egg yolks**

½ cup **sugar**

2 teaspoons **lemon zest, finely minced**

¼ cup **fresh lemon juice**

2 tablespoons **cold butter, cut in pieces**

*****COUNTRY CREAM*****

1 cup **whipping cream**

2 tablespoons **sugar**

¼ cup **sour cream**

½ teaspoon **vanilla extract**

Preheat oven to 375°F.

Sift together the flour, sugar, soda, baking powder, salt and nutmeg into a large bowl. Cut in the butter with a pastry cutter or rub together with your hands until the texture is like coarse crumbs (just like making a pie crust).

In a separate bowl, mix together the egg yolk and buttermilk. Make a well in the center of the dry ingredients and pour the liquid into it. Combine with a few swift strokes. Dough should form a ball and all flour should be incorporated. Do not overmix.

Divide dough into 2 balls and place pieces of dough on a lightly floured surface. With lightly floured hands pat each piece into a 5-inch wide, 3/4-inch thick circle. Carefully place oj a baking sheet and cut each one into 6 wedges, sides still touching.

In a small bowl whisk the egg white, then brush the scones lightly with it and sprinkle liberally with sugar. Bake in the preheated oven for about 30 minutes, until cooked through and scones are golden. Cool slightly before serving.

Serve with Lemon Curd, Country Cream and fresh berries. Makes 12 scones.

Lemon Curd:

In a large metal bowl, place the whole eggs, egg yolks, sugar, lemon zest and lemon juice. Place bowl over a pan of simmering water (bowl not touching the water). Vigorously whisk with a wire whisk. Cook, whisking continuously until nicely thickened like a pie filling, about 4 minutes.

Remove from the heat and whisk in the butter. Do not overcook the mixture or it will curdle. Let cool to room temperature then refrigerate until needed. Makes 1 1/2 cups.

Country Cream: Combine cream and sugar and whip until soft peaks form. Add sour cream and vanilla and gently whisk in. Do not overwhip. Refrigerate. Makes 2 heaping cups.

CLASSIC BAKING-POWDER BISCUITS

Servings: --
Source: Scone Greats

- 2 cups **all-purpose flour**
- 2 teaspoons **baking powder**
- ½ teaspoon **baking soda**
- 1 teaspoon **fine sea salt**
- 8 tablespoons (1 stick) cold **unsalted butter, cut into ¼-inch dice**
- ⅔ cups **milk**
- **Whipped butter for serving (optional)**
- **Warmed maple syrup for serving (optional)**

Scone Greats

Preheat an oven to 450°F. Lightly butter a baking sheet.

In a large bowl, sift together the flour, baking powder, baking soda and salt. With your fingertips, rub the butter into the flour until the mixture resembles coarse meal, handling it as little as possible. Stir in the milk and blend with a spoon just until all the liquid has been absorbed. With lightly floured hands, work the dough briefly until it barely holds together in a flaky ball.

Place the dough on a lightly floured work surface. Roll or pat the dough out into a round about 1/2 inch thick. With a 2-inch biscuit cutter or the rim of a glass, cut out as many rounds as possible. Gather up the scraps, work into a cohesive ball, reroll and cut out more rounds. Do not reroll the dough more than once or you will end up with tough biscuits.

Transfer the biscuits to the prepared baking sheet and bake until golden brown, about 15 minutes. Serve immediately with whipped butter and warm maple syrup.

Comments: The key to making featherlight biscuits and scones is minimal handling of the flaky, crumbly dough. You may think the dough needs more kneading to hold together, but the less you work it, the lighter the result will be. When adding the butter, work quickly so it does not melt into the dough before the biscuits go in the oven. If it becomes soft, the biscuits will be tough. Shape the dough on a lightly floured surface, gently pressing and patting it into a thick circle.

CORNMEAL-RAISIN SCONES

5 servings
Source: Scone Greats

⅔ cup **all-purpose flour**

¼ cup **yellow cornmeal**

3 tablespoons **sugar**

1 teaspoon **baking powder**

¼ teaspoon **baking soda**

⅛ teaspoon **salt**

1 tablespoon **chilled stick margarine**

cut into small pieces

2 tablespoons **golden raisins**

⅓ cup **low-fat buttermilk**

1 **egg, lightly beaten**

Vegetable cooking spray

Combine the first 6 ingredients in a bowl, and cut in margarine with a pastry blender or 2 knives until mixture resembles fine meal. Add the raisins, and toss well.

Combine buttermilk and egg, and add to dry ingredients, stirring just until dry ingredients are moistened (dough will be sticky).

Spoon dough evenly into 5 mounds on a baking sheet coated with cooking spray. Bake at 375 degrees for 18 minutes or until golden. Yield: 5 scones (serving size: 1 scone).

CRANBERRY-ORANGE SCONES

12 servings
Source: Scone Greats

1 cup **all-purpose flour**

1 cup **sifted cake flour**

⅔ cup **sugar**

2 teaspoons **baking powder**

½ teaspoon **baking soda**

¼ teaspoon **salt**

3 tablespoons **chilled stick margarine**

cut into small pieces

¾ cup **frozen cranberries, thawed and halved**

2 teaspoons **grated orange rind**

¾ cup **plain nonfat yogurt**

Vegetable cooking spray

2 teaspoons **sugar**

Combine first 6 ingredients in a bowl; cut in margarine with a pastry blender or 2 knives until mixture resembles coarse meal. Add cranberries and orange rind; toss well. Add yogurt, stirring just until dry ingredients are moistened (dough will be sticky).

Turn the dough out onto a lightly floured surface, and with floured hands, knead 4 or 5 times. Pat dough into an 8-inch circle on a baking sheet coated with cooking spray.

Cut dough into 12 wedges (do not separate the wedges). Sprinkle 2 teaspoons sugar over the dough.

Bake at 450°F for 12 minutes or until golden. Yield: 1 dozen (serving size: 1 scone).

CRAVINGS SCONES

1 servings
Source: Scone Greats

¼ cup **butter**	1 Dash **salt**
⅓ cup **plus 1 tablespoon sugar**	1 Dash **cinnamon**
1 ⅔ cups **pastry flour**	½ cup **heavy whipping cream**
¼ cup **sour cream**	⅔ cup **raisins, optional**
2 ½ tablespoons **baking powder**	

In bowl blend butter and sugar until pale in color. Add pastry flour, sour cream, baking powder, salt and cinnamon, mixing until blended. Add whipping cream and blend well. Fold in raisins.

Gather dough into ball and turn out onto lightly floured surface.

Press or roll out to 1-inch thickness in large rectangle or circle and cut with 2 1/4-inch round cutter. Place cut dough rounds on baking sheet. Bake at 300 degrees 22 minutes. Makes 8 scones.

CRYSTALLIZED GINGER SCONES

Servings: --
Source: Scone Greats

- 2 cups **all-purpose flour**
- ¼ cup **sugar**
- 3 teaspoons **baking powder**
- ½ teaspoon **salt**
- 8 tablespoons **(1 stick) chilled unsalted butter, cut into small pieces**
- ⅓ cup **chopped crystallized ginger**
- 1 **egg**
- ½ cup **heavy cream**

Preheat an oven to 350°F. Lightly grease a scone pan.

In the bowl of a food processor, combine the flour, sugar, baking powder and salt and pulse to combine. Add the butter and pulse until the mixture resembles pea-size crumbs. Transfer to a large bowl, add the crystallized ginger and stir to mix.

In a small bowl, whisk together the egg and cream until blended and add to the flour mixture. Using a fork, stir to form large, moist clumps of dough.

Turn the dough out onto a lightly floured surface and press with your hands until the dough comes together. Roll out the dough, flouring as needed, into a 10-inch round about 3/4 inch thick. Cut into 8 equal-size wedges and press each wedge into a well of the prepared pan. Bake until the scones are golden, about 25 minutes.

Invert the pan onto a wire rack and lift off the pan. Let the scones cool for 10 minutes before serving.

Scone Greats

CURRANT SCONES

18 servings
Source: Scone Greats

2 cups **Unbleached All-Purpose Flour**

1 tablespoon **Baking powder**

6 ounces **Butter, very soft**

3 tablespoons **Sugar**

½ cup **Currants**

2 **Eggs, lightly beaten**

⅓ cup **Milk, or Sour Cream**

Sift together flour, baking powder and salt into a large bowl. Break butter into 1 oz pieces and scatter into flour. For the lightest scones, don't pinch the butter and flour together as when making biscuits. Scoop up a handful of flour and butter and very, very lightly run your thumb across your fingers, allowing the flour to sift through. At first, it will seem as if nothing is happening, but within 2 minutes the mixture will resemble fine crumbs.

Add sugar, currants and eggs. Lightly fold into the flour mixture with your hands. Start with about 1/4 cup milk and add a bit at a time, folding and mixing to make a soft dough. Turn the dough out onto a lightly floured board. Do not knead; just it out into a rectangle about 1" thick. cut it into 2" diamonds or squares. Put the scones on a lightly greased baking sheet. Bake at 425°F for 10 minutes, or until lightly browned and puffed.

Per Scone: Calories: 134, Protein: 2 g, Carbohydrate: 15 g, Fat: 8 g, Saturated Fat: 5 g, Cholesterol: 40 mg, Sodium: 223 mg, Fiber: 1 g.

DOUBLE CHOCOLATE SCONES

1 servings
Source: Scone Greats

Chapter 1: A–M

- 3 cups **all-purpose flour**
- ¼ cup **granulated sugar**
- 4 teaspoons **baking powder**
- ¼ teaspoon **salt**
- ½ cup **butter or margarine**
- **3 large eggs**
- ½ cup **milk**
- ¾ cups **mini chocolate chips, divided**
- 1 tablespoon **grated orange peel**
- ¼ cup **white chocolate chips**

Preheat oven to 450F. Grease a large cookie sheet. Stir the flour, sugar, baking powder, and salt in a large bowl to mix well. Use a pastry blender or two knives to cut in the butter until coarse crumbs form.

Beat the eggs and milk in a small bowl with a wire whisk or a fork; when thoroughly blended, stir, along with 1/2 cup of the mini chocolate chips and the orange peel into the flour mixture just until blended.

Shape the dough with lightly floured hands into an 8-inch round on the prepared cookie sheet; dust with flour.

Score the top of the dough into 8 wedges with a sharp knife. Bake for 20 to 25 minutes until golden. Cool completely on a wire rack.

Meanwhile, stir the remaining 1/4 cup of mini chocolate chips and the white chocolate chips in separate small, heavy saucepans over very low heat until melted and smooth.

Drizzle each chocolate from the tip of spoon in random lines over the top of the scones. Let stand for 15 minutes to set the chocolate.

Cut the scones into wedges along the score lines. Makes 8 scones.

Scone Greats

DRIED CHERRY SCONES

12 servings
Source: Scone Greats

2 cups **cake flour**
2 cups **all-purpose flour**
4 teaspoons **baking powder**
½ cup **granulated sugar**
¼ teaspoon **salt**
4 ounces (1/2 cup) **butter,** chilled and cut up

1 large **egg, beaten**
¾ cups **milk**
4 ounces (about 3/4 cup) dried tart cherries
Light cream (or half-and-half) and granulated sugar

In a food processor, combine cake and all-purpose flour, baking powder, sugar and salt. Add butter, egg and milk; pulse until dough starts to come together. Empty dough onto a lightly floured board and knead lightly, folding in dried cherries at the same time.

Gently form dough into a smooth 10-inch circle about 1 inch thick. With a large knife, cut dough into 12 pie shaped wedges. Brush each lightly with cream and dust with sugar.

Place on lightly greased cookie sheet. Bake in a preheated 375°F oven about 20 minutes, or until lightly browned. Serve warm.

DRIED FRUIT CREAM SCONES

1 servings
Source: Scone Greats

---SCONES---
2 cups **All-purpose flour**
1 tablespoon **Baking powder**
½ teaspoon **Salt**

¼ cup **Sugar**
½ cup **Chopped dried fruit** (apricots, prunes, etc)
¼ cup **Golden raisins**

Chapter 1: A–M

1 ¼ cups **Heavy cream**

GLAZE tb Butter, melted Sugar

Preheat oven to 425°F Use an ungreased baking sheet.

Combine the flour, baking powder, salt, and sugar in a bowl, stirring with a fork to mix well. Add the dried fruit and raisins. Still using a fork, stir in the cream and mix until the dough holds together in a rough mass (the dough will be quite sticky).

Lightly flour a board and transfer the dough to it. Knead the dough or 9 times. into a circle about 10 inches round. For the glaze, spread the butter over the top and side of the circle of dough and sprinkle sugar on top. Cut the circle into 12 wedges and place each piece on the baking sheet, allowing about an inch between pieces.

Bake for about 15 minutes, or until golden brown.

DRIED TART CHEERY SCONES

8 servings
Source: Scone Greats

3 cups + 3 T **flour**	½ cup **Sugar**
6 ½ teaspoons **Baking powder**	½ cup **Chilled butter, cut up**
10 teaspoons **Milk**	1 **Egg, beaten**
½ cup **Dried tart cherries, cut up**	1 teaspoon **Orange or lemon rind;grated**

Preheat oven to 350°F. Lightly grease baking sheet. Stir together the flour, sugar and baking powder. Cut in butter until mixture resembles crumbs. (A food processor works great.) Stir in dried cherries and grated rind. Combine milk and egg. Mix into dry ingredients, gather

Scone Greats

dough into a ball.

Roll dough out 1/2" thick onto a lightly floured surface. Cut into 3" circles with a sharp knife or biscuit cutter. (A glass does not work well because it crimps the edges and they will not rise as well.) Arrange on a baking sheet, 1" apart. Bake until firm to touch, about 20 minutes. Serve warm.

ENGLISH CRUMPETS

4 servings
Source: Scone Greats

4 ounces **All-purpose flour**	½ pint **Warm milk and water**
4 ounces **Bread flour**	1 tablespoon **Vegetable oil**
2 teaspoons **Salt**	½ teaspoon **Bicarbonate of soda**
¼ ounce **Fresh yeast**	¼ pint **Warm water**
1 teaspoon **Sugar**	

Sift the flours and salt into a warm bowl. Cream the yeast with the sugar. Add the warmed milk and water, then the oil. Stir into the flour to make a batter, and beat vigorously until smooth and elastic. Cover the bowl, put in a warm place and leave it until the mixture rises and the surface is full of bubbles (about 1 1/2 hours). Break it down by beating with a wooden spoon.

Cover and leave in a warm place to prove for another 30 minutes. -- To cook the crumpets, heat and grease the bakestone lightly. Grease 5 or 6 crumpet rings (3-3 /2 inches) (or scone cutters) and put them on the bakestone to heat. Cook as many crumpets as possible at a time, as the batter will not stay bubbly for long. -- Put 1/2 inch deep of batter into each ring. Cook gently for 7 - 10 minutes, or until the surface sets and is full of tiny bubbles. Using an oven glove for protection, lift off the ring, and if the base of the crumpet is pale gold, flip it over and cook for another 3 minutes until the other side is

Chapter 1: A–M

just colored.

If the crumpet batter is set but sticks slightly in the ring, push it out gently with the back of a wooden spoon. Wipe, grease and heat the rings for each batch of crumpets. If serving immediately, wrap the crumpets in a cloth and keep warm between batches. Butter generously and serve at once. If reheating, toast the crumpets under the grill, cooking the smooth surface first and then the top so that the butter will melt into the holes.

ENGLISH SCONES

1 servings
Source: Scone Greats

1 cup **self-rising flour**

⅓ cup **sugar**

¼ teaspoon **baking soda**

1 **Dash salt**

⅓ cup **currants**

½ cup **unsalted butter, cut up**

1 **egg**

1 **egg yolk**

¼ cup **buttermilk**

1 teaspoon **vegetable shortening**

Combine flour, sugar, baking soda, salt and currants in bowl. Work in butter until crumbly.

Mix egg, egg yolk and buttermilk with lard and mix lightly but thoroughly into flour mixture. Drop by rounded tablespoons onto greased baking sheet.

Bake at 350°F 12 to 15 minutes or until pale golden. Makes 12 scones.

ENGLISH SCONES

1 servings
Source: Scone Greats

- 1/4 cup **dried currants**
- 1 tablespoon **brandy**
- 1/2 teaspoon **grated orange peel**
- 2 cups **all-purpose flour**
- 6 tablespoons **sugar**
- 1 tablespoon **baking powder**
- 1/4 teaspoon **salt**
- 1/2 cup **butter or margarine**
- 1/2 cup **buttermilk**

1. In a small microwave-safe bowl, mix currants, brandy, and orange peel. Heat in a microwave oven at full power (100%) just until warm, 15 to 20 seconds.

2. In another bowl, mix 2 cups flour, 6 tablespoons sugar, baking powder, and salt. With a pastry blender, cut in 1/2 cup butter until no lumps are larger than 1/4 inch. Stir in currant mixture.

3. Add 1/2 cup buttermilk; stir just enough to evenly moisten dough. If dough is crumbly, sprinkle a little more buttermilk over mixture and stir. Pat dough into a ball and knead in bowl just until dough holds together.

4. Set dough on a lightly buttered 12- by 15-inch baking sheet. Flatten into a 1/2-inch-thick round. With a floured knife, cut round in quarters or eighths, leaving wedges in place. Brush dough with about 2 teaspoons buttermilk and sprinkle with about 1/2 teaspoon sugar.

5. Bake scones in a 400° oven until golden brown, 20 to 25 minutes. Transfer to a rack. Serve warm or cool. Break round into wedges.

Chapter 1: A-M

ENGLISH SCONES

Servings: --
Source: Scone Greats

2 cups **all-purpose flour**

2 teaspoons **cream of tartar**

1 teaspoon **baking soda**

1 teaspoon **sugar**

½ teaspoon **salt**

4 tablespoons (1/2 stick) chilled **unsalted butter, cut into pieces**

¾ cups **milk**

Preheat an oven to 450°F. Lightly grease a baking sheet with solid vegetable shortening.

In a food processor, combine the flour, cream of tartar, baking soda, sugar and salt. Pulse to combine. Add the butter and use on-off pulses until the mixture resembles coarse meal. Transfer to a bowl.

Alternatively, in a bowl, stir together the dry ingredients. Then, using a pastry blender, cut in the butter until the mixture resembles coarse meal.

Make a well in the center of the flour mixture and pour in the milk. Using a fork, mix together until a soft elastic dough forms.

Turn out the dough onto a lightly floured work surface and knead 5 or 6 times until the dough is smooth. Roll out about 3/4 inch thick. Using a scallop-edged cookie cutter 3 inches in diameter, cut out rounds. Transfer to the prepared baking sheet.

Bake the scones until they rise and are golden brown on top, about 10 minutes. Serve hot.

Comments: Serve these fine scones with strawberry jam or a berry butter. If you like, add no more than 1/2 cup chopped plumped dried apricots, whole raisins, chopped crystallized ginger or semisweet chocolate morsels to the dough just before kneading. Fresh blueberries, dried cranberries, or chopped walnuts or pecans are also good additions.

FIVE-FRUIT GRANOLA SCONES

6 servings
Source: Scone Greats

2 cups **All-purpose flour**

⅓ cup **Granulated sugar, divided**

1 tablespoon **Baking powder**

½ teaspoon **Salt**

¼ cup **Butter or margarine**

1 cup **Granola**

16 ounces **Fruit cocktail in juice, dra**

2 **Eggs, beaten**

Preheat oven to 375 degrees; grease a baking sheet. Combine the flour, 1/4 cup sugar, baking powder and salt in a large bowl. Cut in the butter with a pastry blender or knives until the mixture resembles coarse crumbs; stir in the granola. Stir in the fruit cocktail and eggs; blend just until moistened.

Place the dough on a lightly floured surface. Roll out the dough into a 7-inch circle with a lightly floured rolling pin; place on the baking sheet. Sprinkle the remaining sugar over the top. Bake for 45 minutes, or until a toothpick inserted in the center comes out clean. Cut into 6 wedges. Remove from the baking sheet. Cool on a wire rack for 10 minutes. Serve warm or cool completely.

GINGERBREAD SCONES

8 servings
Source: Scone Greats

2 cups **Flour**

3 tablespoons **Brown sugar**

2 teaspoons **Baking powder**

1 teaspoon **Ground ginger**

Chapter 1: A–M

½ teaspoon **Baking soda**

½ teaspoon **Salt**

½ teaspoon **Ground cinnamon**

¼ cup **Butter**

1 **Beaten egg yolk**

⅓ cup **Molasses**

¼ cup **Milk**

1 **Slightly beaten egg white**

Coarse sugar (optional)

1 **Recipe Nutmeg Whipped Cream**

FOR THE NUTMEG WHIPPED CREAM 1/2 c Whipping cream tb Sugar 1/4 ts Finely shredded orange peel 1/4 ts Vanilla 1/8 ts Ground nutmeg

For the scones:

In a large mixing bowl, combine the flour, brown sugar, baking powder, ground ginger, baking soda, salt and cinnamon. Using a pastry cutter, cut in the butter until the mixture resembles coarse crumbs. Make a well in the center. In a small mixing bowl, stir together the egg yolk, molasses, and milk; add all at once to the center of the flour mixture. With a fork, stir until combined (mixture seem dry).

Turn dough onto a lightly floured surface. Quickly knead dough for –12 strokes or until nearly smooth. of lightly roll dough into a 7" circle. Cut into 8 wedges. Arrange wedges on an ungreased baking sheet about 1 inch apart. Brush with egg white and sprinkle with coarse sugar if desired.

Bake at 400°F for 12–15 minutes or till lightly brown. Cool scones on a wire rack for 20 minutes. Serve warm with Nutmeg Whipped Cream if desired.

Nutritional info per serving: 223 calories; 7 gm total fat (4 gm sat. fat); 43 mg chol; 286 mg sodium; 37 gm carbo; 1 gm fiber; 4 gm pro.

To freeze: Cool scones completely and wrap tightly in foil; place in freezer bags. Freeze for up to 3 months. Place frozen, foil-wrapped scones in a 300°F oven and heat for 15-20 minutes or until warm (10-15 minutes if thawed).

For the Nutmeg Whipped Cream:

In a chilled small mixer bowl, combine all of the ingredients. Beat with chilled beaters of an electric mixer on medium speed until soft peaks form. Serve immediately or cover and chill until needed, up to hours. Makes 1 cup.

Nutritional info per 2 Tbsp: 58 calories; 6 gm total fat (3 gm sat fat); 20 mg chol; 6 mg sodium; 2 gm carbo; 0 gm fiber; 0 gm prot.

GIRDLE SCONES

1 servings
Source: Scone Greats

3 ½ cups **Flour;all purpose***	¼ cup **Shortening or lard**
6 tablespoons **Baking powder**	1 **Egg**
1 teaspoon **-salt**	1 ½ cups **Milk**
1 tablespoon **Sugar;granulated**	

Heat flat cast iron pan on low heat for 10 to 15 minutes or until hot. (To test, sprinkle with a little flour; if it browns in 10 to 15 seconds, the pan is hot enough.)

Meanwhile in a large mixing bowl, stir flour, baking powder, salt and sugar; with fingertips, rub in shortening or lard till crumbly. Whisk egg with 1 cup of the milk. Make a well in the centre of the dry ingredients; pour in the liquid. With wooden spoon, stir to make soft, but not sticky dough, adding more milk as needed.

Turn out onto floured board, knead 3 or 4 times. or roll to no more than 1/4 – 1/2 inch. With sharp knife, cut into small triangles. Place a few at a time on pan; cook, rotating scones occasionally for 5 to 6 minutes or until bottoms are browned. Serve hot.

GRIDDLE SCONES

16 servings
Source: Scone Greats

3 cups **Flour**

1 ½ teaspoons **Salt**

1 ½ teaspoons **Baking Soda**

1 ½ teaspoons **Cream of Tartar**

1 teaspoon **Sugar**

1 tablespoon **Butter**

1 ½ cups **Buttermilk**

Sift all of the dry ingredients together into a bowl. By hand, rub the butter into the flour, making small cornmeal-like granules. Add buttermilk all at once. Working quickly but gently, mix with a dinner knife (spoons overwork the dough, making a tough scone) until the dough is just barely mixed. Add a little more buttermilk if necessary, but don't make the dough sticky.

Divide the dough into quarters. On a floured board, roll out each quarter into a circle 1/4" thick. Cut each circle into quarters. Bake the scones in batches on a medium-hot (350°F) lightly greased griddle for a few minutes, until lightly golden. Turn and cook the other side. Now brown all the edges in turn by standing the triangles up and leaning them against each other for about 30 seconds. As the scones come off the griddle, cool in a tea towel until ready to use.

HAMBURGER PETAL PIE

1 servings
Source: Scone Greats

150 g **chopped onion**

150 g **chopped green pepper**

Scone Greats

½ **clove garlic, crushed**	1 **pepper**
30 **vegetable oil**	15 **worcestershire sauce**
800 g **hamburger**	30 **flour**
100 **water**	1 **egg, slightly beaten**
5 **salt**	500 g **canned biscuits**

Saute the onion, green pepper and garlic in the oil until tender then add the beef and cook until brown all over. Dump out the grease and add about 100 ml of water. Add the Worcestershire sauce, salt, pepper and flour. Simmer until the juice thickens. Separate the biscuits and brush the edges with the egg. Put the biscuits against the sides and bottom of a pie plate so it is completely covered.

Stir the rest of the egg into the meat mixture and then spoon the meat into the pie shell. If you wish you can garnish with a few tomato wedges. Bake in a pre-heated oven at 235 C for about 8 to 10 minutes. The biscuits should be slightly browned.

HERB SCONES

4 servings
Source: Scone Greats

½ lb. **Mealy potatoes**	½ teaspoon **Dried dill**
4 tablespoons **Flour**	¼ teaspoon **Savory**
¼ teaspoon **Salt**	¼ teaspoon **Marjoram**
4 tablespoons **Oil**	¼ teaspoon **Powdered sage**
2 tablespoons **Chopped parsley**	**Oil for frying**

Boil or bake the potatoes, then pass through a foodmill. Mix the flour, salt, oil & herbs with the potatoes.

On a floured board, roll this dough to a thickness of about 1/4 inch.

Cut into triangles 3 or inches wide. Fry in very hot oil on both sides until light golden.

HERB SCONES

9 servings
Source: Scone Greats

2 cups **Flour**

1 teaspoon **Cream of tartar**

½ teaspoon **Baking soda**

½ teaspoon **Salt**

1 tablespoon **Dried herbs, your choice**

¼ cup **Grated cheddar cheese**

4 tablespoons **Unsalted butter**

¾ cups **Milk**

Note; Be sure to use chilled butter. In addition, work rapidly after the flour and liquid have been mixed.

Preheat oven to 450°F. Sift all of the dry ingredients together into a bowl. Add the herbs and cheese. Using a pastry cutter, cut in the chilled butter until the mixture looks like coarse crumbs. Make a well in the center, and pour in the milk, blending rapidly to form a soft dough. Do not overmix.

Turn the dough out onto a floured board and or roll out to a 1/2-inch thickness. Using the rim of a glass or 3-inch biscuit cutter, cut into rounds and place them on a greased cookie sheet. Bake for 10 to 12 minutes, or until lightly browned. Serve immediately, split open; or let cool on wire racks and freeze in airtight bags. Reheat frozen scones in an oven at 325°F for about 10 minutes. Each serving contains 161 calories and 6 grams of fat.

JAMMER CREAM SCONES

1 servings
Source: Scone Greats

2 cups **all-purpose flour**	¼ cup **butter or margarine**
1 tablespoon **baking powder**	2 **large eggs**
3 tablespoons **sugar**	⅓ cup **whipping cream**
¼ teaspoon **salt**	¼ cup **raspberry jam**

1. In a bowl, mix 2 cups flour, baking powder, 2 tablespoons sugar, and salt.

2. Cut 1/4 cup butter into chunks; add to bowl. With your fingers or a pastry blender, rub or cut in butter until dough forms pieces no larger than small peas.

3. In a small bowl, beat eggs with cream to blend; set aside 1 tablespoon. Add remaining liquid to flour mixture and stir with a fork just until dough is evenly moistened and sticks together.

4. Scrape dough onto a lightly floured board; turn over to coat with flour.

5. To knead, gently slide your fingers under side of dough opposite you, and lift and fold about half the dough over the portion on the board. Press down gently and push slightly forward.

6. Rotate the dough 90° so a pointed end is in front of you. Again slide your fingers under the farthest point and lift and fold about half the dough over the portion on the board. Press down gently and push slightly forward again. Keep turning and kneading just until dough forms a neat ball, 3 or 4 more times.

7. In a buttered, floured 10- by 15-inch pan, pat dough into a 1-inch-thick round. With a floured sharp knife, cut round into 6 to 8 equal wedges and leave in place.

8. Dust your thumb with flour and push it straight down and almost through the middle of the wide end of each wedge, wiggling to make a hole that is 1/2 to 3/4 inch wide. Divide jam equally among the holes. Brush reserved egg mixture over dough and sprinkle evenly with 2 to 3 teaspoons sugar.

9. Bake in a 375° oven until richly browned, about 25 minutes (350° in a convection oven). Serve hot.

MAKES: 6 to 8 servings

LEMON AND LIME CURD

1 servings
Source: Scone Greats

6 medium lemons	**4 eggs, beaten**
3 medium limes, (or 4)	**½ cup butter or margarine, cut up**
1 ½ cups sugar	

Wash lemons and limes and dry them. Finely shred lemon peels to make 1/4 cup. Avoid getting the white pith in with the rind.

Squeeze enough juice from lemons and limes to make 1 1/3 cups total.

In a heavy 1 quart saucepan combine the juice and sugar.

Stir in the eggs, margarine and 1/4 cup lemon peel. Cook and stir constantly over medium heat (do not boil) until mixture coats metal spoon.

Takes about 8 minutes. Remove from heat and put in jars. Keep in refrigerator.

Scone Greats

Makes 3 - 1 cup gifts.

NOTES : Gift label: British teatime spread. Use as a filling for cakes and tarts or serve with hot muffins or scones. Optional: Omit lime. Use 1 1/3 cups lemon juice.

LEMON CREAM SCONES

8 servings
Source: Scone Greats

2 cups **all-purpose flour**

⅓ cup **sugar, granulated**

1 teaspoon **baking powder**

¼ teaspoon **salt**

½ cup **golden raisins**

1 teaspoon **lemon peel, finely grated**

1 cup **whipping cream**

2 tablespoons **water to 4 as needed**

Preheat oven to 375°F.

In a bowl, combine flour, sugar, baking powder and salt. Stir in raisins and lemon peel.

With a fork, stir in whipping cream and enough water as needed until it all comes together into a rough mass.

On a lightly-floured surface, knead dough 5 to 6 times. Place on greased cookie sheet and pat into an 8-inch circle.

With a sharp knife cut half-way through dough to mark 12 pie-shaped wedges.

Bake 20-30 minutes until golden brown.

Chapter 1: A–M

Remove to a wire rack to cool.

Cut into wedges while still warm or cool completely before cutting.

Serve warm or at room temperature.

Makes 12 scones.

LEMON CURD #2

1 servings
Source: Scone Greats

½ cup **Butter**

½ cup **Sugar, or**

⅓ cup **Honey**

4 **Eggs**

1 **Egg Yolk**

½ cup **Fresh Lemon Juice**

3 tablespoons **Lemon Peel, grated**

Melt butter in a double boiler over simmering water. Add sugar; stir until dissolved. Using a wire whisk, beat in eggs, egg yolk, lemon juice and peel.

Cook over low heat, stirring, until mixture thickens. Do not overcook, as curd curdle and separate. Remove from hot water. Cool 5 minutes. Pour into containers and seal. Refrigerate for up to 2 weeks. Serve with muffins, scones, english muffins, or toast.

LEMON ECLAIR FILLING

1 servings
Source: Scone Greats

2 cups **sugar**

½ cup **butter**

Scone Greats

3 eggs, well beaten	**3 lemons**
½ cup **water**	

Grate rinds of lemons with a grater or zester. Squeeze the lemons and strain out seeds; use all the lemon juice in recipe. Cream the butter and sugar thoroughly; add the eggs and mix well.

Add the water, lemon juice and grated rind. Cook in top of double boiler until thick. Chill.

Use this lemon butter as filling for eclairs, scones, or to serve with a plain cake such as angel food or pound cake.

LEMON PECAN SCONES

8 servings
Source: Scone Greats

2 cups **unbleached white flour**	½ cup **chopped pecans**
¼ cup **sugar**	1 ¼ cups **heavy cream**
1 tablespoon **baking powder**	½ teaspoon **lemon extract**
½ teaspoon **salt**	1 tablespoon **melted butter**
grated zest of one lemon	1 tablespoon **sugar**

Preheat oven to 425°F

Combine the flour, sugar, baking powder, and salt in a bowl. Add the lemon zest and pecans. In a measuring cup, stir together heavy cream and lemon extract.

Stir into dry ingredients until dough holds together in a rough mass. Do not over-mix. The dough will be quite sticky. Lightly flour a board and transfer the dough to it.

Knead the dough 8 or 9 times. Pat into two circles about 6 inches round. Brush melted butter over the top and side of the circle of dough and sprinkle the sugar on top.

Cut each circle into 6 wedges and place pieces on an ungreased baking sheet, allowing about an inch between pieces.

Bake at 375 for 15-20 minutes or until golden brown.

LEMON SCONES

8 servings
Source: Scone Greats

2 cups **Flour, sifted**

2 tablespoons **Sugar**

2 tablespoons **Lemon Peel, grated**

2 tablespoons **Baking Powder**

½ teaspoon **Salt**

½ cup **Butter, chilled**

1 **Egg, slightly beaten**

⅔ cups **Buttermilk;** at room temperature

1 teaspoon **Lemon Extract**

¼ cup **Currants, optional**

¼ cup **Almonds, blanched and chopped**

----GLAZE---- 1/2 tb Fresh Lemon Juice tb Sugar

Preheat oven to 425°F. Lightly grease a baking sheet or use nonstick cooking spray. Combine flour, sugar, lemon peel, baking powder and salt. With a pastry blender or food processor, cut butter into flour mixture until the texture of coarse meal. Add egg, 1/3 cup of the buttermilk and lemon extract. Add remaining buttermilk, a tablespoon at a time, if needed, to make a soft dough.

Turn dough onto a lightly floured board and knead in currants and almonds. Divide dough into half. Shape each half into a smooth ball. Press out each ball with your hand into a 6" round. Cut each round into 4 wedges. For glaze, mix lemon juice with sugar, brush over scones. Place on baking sheet 1" apart. Bake in the top third of oven minutes or until golden brown. Remove from pan and cool slightly on wire rack. Serve warm. Reheat on oven rack at lowest position under broiler for 2 minutes.

LOW-FAT DATE SCONES

10 servings
Source: Scone Greats

- 1 ½ cups **all-purpose flour**
- ½ cup **whole-wheat flour**
- ¼ cup **unprocessed wheat bran**
- ¼ cup **firmly packed brown sugar**
- 2 teaspoons **ground cinnamon**
- 1 ½ teaspoons **baking powder**
- 1 ½ teaspoons **baking soda**
- ½ teaspoon **salt**
- 3 tablespoons **chilled stick margarine** cut into small pieces
- ⅔ cup **chopped pitted dates**
- ⅔ cup **vanilla low-fat yogurt**
- 2 **egg whites, lightly beaten**
- **Vegetable cooking spray**

Combine first 8 ingredients in a bowl; cut in margarine with a pastry blender until the mixture resembles coarse meal. Add dates; toss well. Add yogurt and egg whites, stirring just until dry ingredients are moistened (dough will be sticky).

Turn dough out onto a lightly floured surface; with floured hands, knead lightly 3 to 4 times. Pat dough into an 8-inch circle on a baking sheet coated with cooking spray. Cut dough into 10 wedges, cutting into but not through dough.

Bake at 350 degrees for 25 minutes or until loaf sounds hollow when tapped. Yield: 10 scones.

MOIST SPICED APPLE SCONES

8 servings
Source: Scone Greats

2 cups **All-purpose flour**

½ cup **Brown sugar, packed**

2 teaspoons **Baking powder**

½ teaspoon **Ground cinnamon**

¼ teaspoon **Ground nutmeg**

¼ teaspoon **Ground ginger**

⅛ teaspoon **Salt**

2 tablespoons **Butter or margarine**

1 cup **Dried apples, chopped**

½ cup **Unsweetened applesauce**

¼ cup **Buttermilk**

1 **Egg**

--**Topping:**---

1 teaspoon **Granulated sugar**

⅛ teaspoon **Ground cinnamon**

Preheat oven to 375 degrees; spray a large cookie sheet with nonstick cooking spray. In a medium bowl, combine the flour, brown sugar, baking powder, cinnamon, nutmeg, ginger and salt; mix well. Using a pastry blender or fork, cut in the margarine until the mixture resembles coarse crumbs.

Stir in the apples. In a small bowl, combine the applesauce, buttermilk and egg; mix well. Add to the dry ingredients; stir just until moistened. The dough will be sticky. Place the dough on the cookie sheet. With wet fingers, shape it into an 8-inch circle about 3/4-inch thick. In a small bowl, combine sugar and cinnamon; sprinkle over the top of the dough.

With a sharp knife, score the top surface into 8 wedges, cutting about 1/4-inch deep. Bake for 18 to 22 minutes, or until golden brown and a toothpick inserted in the center comes out clean. Cut into wedges.

Scone Greats

Serve warm.

Nutrition Analysis: 240 calories, 4g protein, 45g carbohydrate, 4g fat, mg cholesterol, 170mg sodium, g fiber.

Chapter 2
N–Z

OAT SCONES WITH APPLE-PEAR BUTTER

12 servings
Source: Scone Greats

- 1 cup **All-purpose flour, unbleache or whole wheat pastry flou**
- 1 cup **Rolled oats**
- 3 tablespoons **Light brown sugar, packed**
- ¼ teaspoon **Salt**
- 6 tablespoons **Unsalted butter, cold cut into pieces**
- 1 **Egg**
- ½ cup **Half and half**

- --Apple pear butter:---
- ¼ lb. **Dried apples, unsulphered**
- 2 ounces **Dried pears**
- 2 cups **Apple juice, unsweetened or pear juice**
- 2 teaspoons **Ground cinnamon**
- 1 teaspoon **Ground allspice**
- ½ teaspoon **Ground cloves**
- 2 tablespoons **Unsalted butter**

Preheat oven to 375 degrees; grease a baking sheet or line with parchment. Combine the flour and oats in the workbowl of a food processor and process until the oats are ground. In a medium bowl, combine the flour mixture, brown sugar, baking powder and salt.

Cut in the butter with a fork or a heavy-duty electric mixer until the mixture resembles coarse crumbs. In a small bowl, whisk together the egg and half and half. Add to the dry mixture and stir until a sticky dough is formed. Turn the dough out onto a lightly floured surface and knead about 6 times, just until the dough holds together. the dough into a 3/4-inch thick round about 8 inches in diameter.

Cut out the scones with a 2-inch biscuit cutter to make 12 to 14 smaller scones. Place the scones about 1 inch apart on the baking sheet. Bake for 15 to 18 minutes until crusty and golden brown. Serve immediately, split in half and spread with Apple-Pear Butter. To make Apple-Pear Butter, combine the apples, pears, juice and spices in a heavy saucepan and bring to a boil.

Reduce the heat to a simmer and cook, uncovered, for 30 minutes, stirring occasionally. Remove from the heat, stir in the butter and cool. Puree in a blender or food processor until smooth. Scrape into a spring top glass jar and refrigerate until needed. Makes about 2 cups, keeps for about 2 months.

OATMEAL APPLE CRANBERRY SCONES

12 servings
Source: Scone Greats

2 cups **All-purpose flour**

1 cup **Rolled oats**

⅓ cup **Granulated sugar**

2 teaspoons **Baking powder**

½ teaspoon **Salt**

½ teaspoon **Baking soda**

½ teaspoon **Ground cinnamon**

¾ cups **Natural applesauce, divided**

2 tablespoons **Margarine**

½ cup **Cranberries, coarsely choppe**

½ cup **Peeled apple, chopped**

¼ cup **Skim milk**

¼ cup **Honey, plus**

2 tablespoons **Honey, divided**

Preheat oven to 425 degrees; spray a baking sheet with nonstick cooking spray. In a large bowl, combine the flour, oats, sugar, baking powder, salt, baking soda and cinnamon. Add 1/2 cup applesauce and the margarine; cut in with a pastry blender or fork until the mixture resembles coarse crumbs. Stir in the cranberries and apple. In a small bowl, combine the milk and 1/4 cup honey. Add to the flour mixture; stir together until the dough forms a ball.

Turn the dough out onto a well-floured surface; knead 10 to 12 times. Shaping the dough into an 8-inch circle. Place on the baking sheet. Use the tip of a knife to score the dough into 12 wedges. In another small bowl, combine the remaining 1/4 cup applesauce and 2 tablespoons honey. Brush the mixture over the top of the dough. Bake for 12 to 15 minutes, or until lightly browned. Immediately remove from the baking sheet; cool on a wire rack for 10 minutes. Serve warm or cool completely. Cut into 12 wedges.

Nutrition Analysis: 170 calories, 2.5g fat, 0mg cholesterol, 200mg sodium.

OLD FASHIONED CREAM SCONES

1 servings
Source: Scone Greats

- 2 cups **Unsifted all purpose flour**
- 3 teaspoons **Baking powder**
- 2 tablespoons **Sugar**
- ½ teaspoon **Salt**
- 4 tablespoons **Butter**
- 2 **Eggs, beaten; see note**
- ⅓ cup **Heavy cream**
- 2 teaspoons **Sugar**

Note: Reserve 1 Tablespoon egg white for brushing on top.

Preheat oven to 400°F.

Combine flour, baking powder, 2 Tablespoons sugar and salt. Cut in butter with your fingers, a fork or two knives. Beat eggs slightly with cream, and stir into flour mixture. Turn out onto a lightly floured surface and knead only until dough sticks together. Divide in two parts.

Rolls each part out into a circle that is 1" thick and 6" in diameter. Cut each circle into = wedges, and put wedges on ungreased baking sheet. Bake for 15 minutes.

OLD FASHIONED SCONES

12 servings
Source: Scone Greats

3 cups **Self-raising flour**

1 teaspoon **Salt**

2 teaspoons **Sugar**

2 ounces (60 g) **Butter**

1 cup **Milk**

Set oven at 450F. Arrange shelf in oven in the top third of the oven.

Sift the flour, salt, and sugar into a bowl, rub in the butter, add milk to make a soft dough. Knead lightly on floured surface, then into a rectangle about 3/4" thick. Cut into squares or rounds. Arrange on a lightly greased tray. Brush with milk to glaze. Bake for - 15 minutes, or until well risen and golden brown.

ORANGE SCONES WITH RASPBERRY FILLING

16 servings
Source: Scone Greats

3 ¼ cups **Flour**

¼ cup **Sugar**

4 teaspoons **Baking powder**

½ teaspoon **Salt**

6 tablespoons **Butter or margarine**

3 **Eggs, beaten**

½ cup **Whipping cream**

1 tablespoon **Grated orange peel**

3 tablespoons **Raspberry preserves**

Icing sugar

RAISIN SCONES

1 servings
Source: Scone Greats

½ teaspoon **Saffron Threads**
¾ cups **Buttermilk (180ml)**
2 cups **Whole wheat flour (260g)**
6 tablespoons **Butter, in pieces (75g)**
4 teaspoons **Baking powder**
½ teaspoon **Salt**
1 tablespoon **Lemon juice**
2 tablespoons **Sugar**
½ teaspoon **Ground cumin**
½ cup **Raisins (120g)**
g **Zest of one large orange**

Cumin and saffron combine here with raisins to make a heavenly version of this popular breakfast bread.

Steep saffron in lemon juice for 20 minutes. Sift together dry ingredients. Cut butter into flour coarsely. Add raisins and zest, mix well. Add saffron to milk, mix well, then add to flour to form dough.

Before lifting dough from work bowl, flour a surface large enough to make about a 9-inch circle. Preheat oven to 450F (232C). With a floured knife blade, cut the dough into 8 wedges. Transfer the dough onto a greased cookie sheet and bake for 15 to 20 minutes until browned and cooked through. Serve warm.

RAISIN SCONES

6 servings
Source: Scone Greats

- 2 cups **Flour**
- 2 teaspoons **Baking powder**
- ½ teaspoon **Baking soda**
- ½ teaspoon **Ground nutmeg**
- 8 tablespoons (1 stick) cold unsalted **butter, cut up**
- 1 cup **Raisins**
- 2 tablespoons **Sugar**
- 1 **Yolk of a large egg**
- ¾ cups **Buttermilk or plain yogurt**
- 1 **White of a large egg**
- Additional **sugar for sprinkling**

Heat oven to 375°F. Put flour, baking powder, soda, nutmeg, and salt into a large bowl. Stir to mix well. Add butter and cut in with a pastry blender or rub in with your fingers, until the mixture looks like fine granules. Add raisins and sugar; toss to distribute evenly.

Add egg yolk to buttermilk in a measuring cup and whisk with a fork to blend. Pour over the flour mixture and stir with a fork until a soft dough forms.

Turn out dough onto a lightly floured surface and give 10-12 kneads. Cut dough in half. Knead each half briefly into a ball; turn smooth side up and into a 6 inch circle. Cut in 6 wedges, but do not separate wedges.

In a small bowl, beat the egg white with a fork until just broken up. Brush to top of each scone with the egg white, and sprinkle lightly with sugar. With a pancake turner, carefully transfer the two cut circles to an ungreased cookie sheet. If necessary, reshape circles so that the 6 wedges in each are touching. This will keep the raisins from burning. 5. Bake 18-22 minutes or until medium brown. Cool on a wire rack. After 5 minutes pull the wedges apart and cover loosely with a dish towel.

Chapter 2: N-Z

Note: Egg white and sugar can be added before freezing the unbaked scones.

VARIATION: Coarse Whole-Wheat Raisin Scones: Replace 1 cup all-purpose flour with 1 cup whole-wheat flour, and add 1/2 cup miller's bran to the flour mixture. Omit nutmeg.

REAL ORANGE AND CURRANT SCONES

18 servings
Source: Scone Greats

1 ½ cups **cake flour**

¼ cup **sugar**

¾ teaspoon **baking powder**

¼ teaspoon **baking soda**

⅛ teaspoon **salt**

6 tablespoons **butter, cut up**

⅓ cup **currants**

1 tablespoon **minced orange zest**

⅓ cup **whipping cream**

2 tablespoons **orange juice**

All-purpose flour, for kneading

1 **egg**

¼ teaspoon **salt**

Mix flour, sugar, baking powder, baking soda and salt. Use pastry blender to cut butter into flour until mixture is crumbly. Stir in currants and zest. Add cream and juice. Stir with fork until flour is moistened; do not overmix.

Knead dough 5 to 6 times until smooth on lightly floured surface. Pat dough until uniformly 1/2-inch thick. Cut out scones with floured 1 3/4-inch cutter. Use dough scraps by gently pressing together.

Scones can be wrapped and refrigerated or frozen; place scones in layers, separated by wax paper, in airtight container. When ready to bake, use scones directly from refrigerator or freezer.

Place on baking sheet (not black steel), spacing 1 inch apart. Whisk together egg and salt. Lightly brush onto scones (some glaze will be unused). Bake at 425 degrees until bottoms are browned and interior is not wet and doughy (separate 1 scone to check), about 8 to 10 minutes.

This recipe yields 16 to 18 scones.

Each of 18 scones: 99 calories; 111 mg sodium; 28 mg cholesterol; 6 grams fat; 11 grams carbohydrates; 1 gram protein; 0.09 gram fiber.

Comments: These scones can be made ahead, completely baked and frozen, or frozen unbaked.

ROSEMARY AND HAM SCONES

4 servings
Source: Scone Greats

- **1 box biscuit mix** = (Jiffy recommended)
- 3 tablespoons **finely-chopped rosemary** - (4 small stems)
- ½ cup **cream**
- A couple pinches **salt**
- 3 pieces **deli-sliced glazed smoked ham** - (abt 2 oz), chopped
- 1 tablespoon **orange zest**
- 2 teaspoons **sugar**

Preheat oven to 375 degrees.

Mix together biscuit mix, rosemary, cream, salt, ham and orange zest. Pile mixture into 4 large mounds or 8 small mounds onto a nonstick cookie sheet. Sprinkle with a little sugar and bake. Bake scones for 10 to 12 minutes for large scones, 7 to 8 minutes for small scones.

This recipe yields 4 servings.

SALMON CAKES SALAD

4 servings
Source: Scone Greats

2 cans **salmon with bones** - (14 oz ea), drained

2 **egg whites**, beaten

⅓ cup **Italian bread crumbs**

1 tablespoon **all-purpose seasoning**

= (Old Bay recommended)

A few drops **hot sauce**

= (Tabasco recommended)

2 tablespoons **chopped flat-leaf parsley**

3 tablespoons **chopped roasted red pepper** - (to 4)

= (1/2 pepper from a jar, drained, then chopped)

Salt, to taste

Freshly-ground black pepper, to taste

1 tablespoon **vegetable oil**

=== SALAD ===

1 head **frissee lettuce**, coarsely chopped

1 **endive**, sliced

1 **romaine heart**, chopped

2 cups **baby spinach leaves** - (abt 1/4 lb)

1 **navel orange**, peeled, chopped

½ small **red onion**, thinly sliced

1 tablespoon **orange zest**

3 tablespoons **red wine vinegar**

¼ cup **extra-virgin olive oil** - (to 1/3)

Salt, to taste

Freshly-ground black pepper, to taste

Rosemary And Ham Scones, (see recipe)

Heat a medium skillet over medium-high heat.

Combine salmon, egg white, bread crumbs, crab boil seasoning, hot sauce, parsley, roasted red pepper and salt and pepper. Form 4 patties, 1-inch thick.

Add vegetable oil to hot pan, 1 turn of the pan. Add patties and cook about 3 minutes on each side until golden brown and cooked through.

Scone Greats

Combine greens, chopped orange and red onion in a salad bowl. Combine orange zest, vinegar and a splash of juice from the zested orange in a small bowl. Whisk in extra-virgin olive oil to desired bite and constituency for dressing. Dress and toss salad.

Season the salad with salt and pepper, to taste then divide among 4 plates. Top salads with warm salmon cakes and serve with Ham and Rosemary Scones or warm pumpernickel bread and butter, as a close-second choice.

This recipe yields 4 servings.

SAUSAGE BALLS - 1

1 servings
Source: Scone Greats

500 g bulk hot sausage

400 g Bisquick

500 g sharp cheddar cheese, grated

Preheat the oven to 190 C. Grate the cheese.

Combine all the ingredients and knead until well mixed. You may need to add a little beef broth to get it to stick together.

Shape into 3-cm balls and place on a cookie sheet or broiler pan.

Bake at 190 C for 25 minutes.

Author's Notes: I got this from my sister who got it from my mother. My mother has been cooking it for a long time.

Don't put too many on a cookie sheet or the grease will fill it up and run off into your oven. These should be served with cocktail sauce.

Chapter 2: N–Z

They are very rich. They can be made ahead and frozen until your party, then warmed before serving. Cooks outside North America should remember that a biscuit is a scone. If you don't have any biscuit mix, you can make some by cutting together of flour, of baking powder, and of vegetable shortening or butter.

SAVORY CHEESE SCONES

12 servings
Source: Scone Greats

2 cups **Flour**

2 teaspoons **Baking powder**

½ teaspoon **Salt**

⅛ teaspoon **Cayenne pepper**

1 ½ cups **Grated cheddar cheese**

3 tablespoons **Parmesan cheese**

⅓ cup **Butter**

⅓ cup **Milk**

2 **Eggs**

Preheat oven to 400°F Combine all dry ingredients, stir in cheeses and toss well. Cut in butter. Combine eggs and milk, add to flour mixture and gently knead to form a stiff dough.

Cut dough ball into halves and each half into an 8" diameter, 1/2" thick circle. Cut into wedges, place wedges on= a baking sheet and bake 15 to 17 minutes, until lightly browned.

SCONES

8 servings
Source: Scone Greats

2 cups **white flour**

4 teaspoons **baking powder**

¼ cup **brown sugar**

½ teaspoon **salt**

Scone Greats

4 tablespoons **butter**
BEAT TOGETHER:
2 **eggs**
1 **egg yolk**
2 teaspoons **vanilla**
½ cup **yogurt or cream**
½ cup **raisins or dried fruit** (optional)

TOPPING – MIX TOGETHER:
1 **egg white**
1 teaspoon **water**
MIX TOGETHER:
3 tablespoons **brown sugar**
1 teaspoon **cinnamon**

Heat oven to 450°F. Grease a cookie sheet with butter. Sift together flour, sugar, salt and baking powder. Cut the cold butter in with a fork or a pastry cutter until well mixed. Do not overwork. Add well-beaten eggs and yolk, and vanilla. Add half the yogurt and then slowly add the rest until it becomes a soft, but manipulatable dough and mix only until blended. Add raisins, currants, dried cranberries or dried fruit, if desired.

For fancy scones, turn dough out onto a floured board and knead briefly, then roll into a 3/4-inch slab. Cut dough into 8 large diamond shapes or triangles. Brush with egg and water mixture then sprinkle with brown sugar and cinnamon mixture. Place on cookie sheet and bake about 15 to 20 minutes.

For the quick method: When dough is completely mixed together, scoop up a large serving spoon of dough and hold in place on the spoon while you dip it in the egg mixture, then the cinnamon mixture. Place on cookie sheet and bake about 15 to 20 minutes.

NOTES : Sweet and fluffy biscuits for tea or breakfast. Traditional English scones have very little sugar in them. This recipe is definitely sweeter, but a nice change from the morning muffin. They can stand on their own without jam.

Chapter 2: N–Z

SCONES

1 servings
Source: Scone Greats

- 2 ½ cups **pastry flour**
- 1 tablespoon **baking powder**
- ½ cup **salted butter, ice cold and cut into pieces**
- 1 cup **raisins, rinsed**
- 6 tablespoons **sugar**
- ⅔ cup **whipping cream**

Combine flour and baking powder in medium bowl.

Work butter into flour mixture with pastry blender, 2 knives or fingers until mixture forms pea-sized pieces.

Add raisins and sugar, and toss with fork to blend. Let stand overnight at room temperature.

Add whipping cream and stir until ingredients begin to hold together.

Place on lightly floured surface and knead gently 10 to 12 times.

Divide dough into 12 pieces and pat into 2 1/2-inch rounds.

Place on ungreased baking sheet so they don't touch each other.

Bake at 425°F degrees until light golden brown, 12 to 15 minutes.

Transfer to paper towel-covered wire rack, cover with paper towel and let cool 30 minutes before serving. Makes: 12 scones.

SCONES

14 servings
Source: Scone Greats

- 3 cups **cake flour, plus more**
- 2 tablespoons **baking powder**

Scone Greats

2 tablespoons **sugar**

¾ teaspoon **salt**

½ cup **butter, cut into cubes**

2 cups **whipping cream**

1 cup **currants**

1 egg yolk, beaten

Devonshire cream and preserves, (optional)

Sift together flour, baking powder, sugar and salt. Use paddle on electric mixer to work butter into flour mixture until mealy. Add whipping cream and currants. Mix on low until dough is smooth, 1 minute.

Turn dough onto floured board and roll out to about 3/4-inch thick. Cut into 2 1/4-inch rounds with pastry cutter or biscuit cutter. Place dough rounds 2 inches apart on baking sheet lined with parchment paper.

Brush with beaten egg yolk and bake at 375°F until golden brown, 18 to 20 minutes. Serve with Devonshire cream and preserves, if desired.

This recipe yields 12 to 14 scones.

Each of 14 scones: 278 calories; 390 mg sodium; 84 mg cholesterol; 20 grams fat; 22 grams carbohydrates; 3 grams protein; 0.32 gram fiber.

SCONES

8 servings
Source: Scone Greats

2 cups **flour**

4 teaspoons **double-acting baking powder**

½ tablespoon **salt**

2 tablespoons **sugar**

½ cup **vegetable shortening**

⅔ cup **milk**

1 large egg, reserve 1 tsp. white

½ cup **currants**

Sift dry ingredients together. Cut shortening into dry ingredients until mixture is crumbly. Beat egg and milk together. Stir quickly into dry ingredients. Stir in currants. Pat out into a round 1/2" thick and cut into wedges.

Place on greased cookie sheet. Beat reserved egg white lightly with 1/2 teaspoon water. Brush on top of scones and sprinkle with additional sugar.

Bake at 450 degrees for 12 to 15 minutes.

SCONES

8 servings
Source: Scone Greats

2 cups **white flour**

4 teaspoons **baking powder**

¼ cup **brown sugar**

½ teaspoon **salt**

4 tablespoons **butter**

BEAT TOGETHER:

2 **eggs**

1 **egg yolk**

2 teaspoons **vanilla**

½ cup **yogurt or cream**

½ cup **raisins or dried fruit (optional)**

TOPPING – MIX TOGETHER:

1 **egg white**

1 teaspoon **water**

MIX TOGETHER:

3 tablespoons **brown sugar**

1 teaspoon **cinnamon**

Heat oven to 450°F. Grease a cookie sheet with butter. Sift together flour, sugar, salt and baking powder. Cut the cold butter in with a fork or a pastry cutter until well mixed. Do not overwork. Add well-beaten eggs and yolk, and vanilla. Add half the yogurt and then slowly add the rest until it becomes a soft, but manipulatable dough and mix only until blended. Add raisins, currants, dried cranberries or dried

Scone Greats

fruit, if desired.

For fancy scones, turn dough out onto a floured board and knead briefly, then roll into a 3/4-inch slab. Cut dough into 8 large diamond shapes or triangles. Brush with egg and water mixture then sprinkle with brown sugar and cinnamon mixture. Place on cookie sheet and bake about 15 to 20 minutes.

For the quick method: When dough is completely mixed together, scoop up a large serving spoon of dough and hold in place on the spoon while you dip it in the egg mixture, then the cinnamon mixture. Place on cookie sheet and bake about 15 to 20 minutes.

NOTES : Sweet and fluffy biscuits for tea or breakfast. Traditional English scones have very little sugar in them. This recipe is definitely sweeter, but a nice change from the morning muffin. They can stand on their own without jam.

SCONES

8 servings
Source: Scone Greats

2 cups **cake flour**

2 teaspoons **baking powder**

¼ cup **sugar, plus**

1 tablespoon **sugar**

½ teaspoon **salt**

6 tablespoons **very cold butter**

2 **eggs**

½ cup **whipping cream, plus**

1 tablespoon **whipping cream**

Grated zest of 1 lemon or orange

½ cup **currants**

Sift together flour, baking powder, 1/4 cup sugar and salt. Cut in butter with pastry blender or 2 knives. Combine eggs, 1/2 cup cream and zest. Make well in center of dry ingredients. Pour in currants and egg mixture. Stir until almost fully incorporated. Place dough on lightly floured surface and knead 5 times; it will be sticky.

Divide dough in half. Place on parchment-paper-lined baking sheet and pat into 2 circles 1 inch thick. Cut each circle into 4 wedges but do not separate. Sprinkling sugar on knife may make dough easier to cut. Brush with remaining 1 tablespoon cream and sprinkle with remaining 1 tablespoon sugar.

Bake at 400 degrees until light golden brown on top, about 20 minutes.

This recipe yields 8 scones.

Each scone: 261 calories; 364 mg sodium; 88 mg cholesterol; 13 grams fat; 31 grams carbohydrates; 4 grams protein; 0.29 gram fiber

---

SCOTTISH ROCK BUNS

6 servings
Source: Scone Greats

- 2 cups **white flour**
- 2 tablespoons **granulated sugar, (or more to taste up to 6 tablespoons)**
- 3 ounces **butter or margarine**
- 1 ½ teaspoons **baking powder**
- ⅜ cup **currants**
- ½ teaspoon **vanilla extract**
- 1 **egg, beaten**
- 2 tablespoons **milk**

Combine flour, sugar, baking powder.

Work the butter into the mixture with your hands, leaving it chunky.

Mix together milk, egg and vanilla, blend into mixture.

Scone Greats

Add currants.

Break off 2 or 2 1/2-inch pieces of the dough and arrange on a dry baking pan.

Bake at 400° until golden brown on top (about 15-20 minutes). Serves 4 to 6

NOTES :

Simple, traditional, basic breakfast pastry. Rock buns are a slightly drier, perhaps tastier, variation of scones. Great the next day.
You might experiment with the sugar and butter content: more butter makes them richer and more scone-like. Instead of currants you can use chopped dry cranberries.

SCOTTISH ROCK BUNS

6 servings
Source: Scone Greats

- 2 cups **white flour**
- 2 tablespoons **granulated sugar, (or more to taste –**
- **up to 6 tablespoons)**
- 3 ounces **butter or margarine**
- 1 ½ teaspoons **baking powder**
- ⅜ cup **currants**
- ½ teaspoon **vanilla extract**
- 1 **egg, beaten**
- 2 tablespoons **milk**

Combine flour, sugar, baking powder. Work the butter into the mixture with your hands, leaving it chunky. Mix together milk, egg and vanilla, blend into mixture. Add currants.

Break off 2 or 2 1/2-inch pieces of the dough and arrange on a dry baking pan. Bake at 400° until golden brown on top (about 15-20

Chapter 2: N-Z

minutes).

Serves 4 to 6

NOTES : Simple, traditional, basic breakfast pastry. Rock buns are a slightly drier, perhaps tastier, variation of scones. Great the next day.

You might experiment with the sugar and butter content: more butter makes them richer and more scone-like. Instead of currants you can use chopped dry cranberries.

SODA SCONES

6 servings
Source: Scone Greats

-----

lb White Flour ts Baking Soda ts Cream of Tartar 1/2 ts Salt tb Margarine c Buttermilk

Preheat oven to 350°F. Sift dry ingredients. Cut in margarine. Add buttermilk a little at a time to make a stiff dough. Knead for two or three minutes. Roll out to 1/2 inch thick on a floured surface.

Cut with a 3-inch biscuit cutter and place on a cookie sheet. Bake 15 minutes. When brown on top, turn and brown the other side.

Makes 6 – 8 scones.

SOUR CHERRY AND VANILLA CREAM SCONES

16 servings
Source: Scone Greats

2 cups **unbleached flour, plus more**

1 cup **cake flour**

2 teaspoons **baking powder**

½ teaspoon **baking soda**

¼ teaspoon **salt**

¾ cup **sugar, plus more**

2 teaspoons **finely-grated orange zest**

¾ cup **very cold butter, cut small chunks**

1 **egg, lightly beaten**

½ teaspoon **vanilla extract**

¾ cup **buttermilk or orange juice, plus more**

1 cup **dried sour cherries**

2 tablespoons **cream**

Combine unbleached and cake flours, baking powder, baking soda, salt, sugar and zest in large bowl. Cut in butter until mixture is grainy and coarse. (Alternatively, in bowl of large food processor, place butter chunks on top of dry ingredients. Pulse to break butter into flour mixture, then move mixture to large bowl.)

Make well in center of dry ingredients and stir in egg, vanilla and buttermilk or orange juice. With a fork, lightly bring mixture in toward center to combine wet and dry ingredients. When slightly combined, fold in cherries. Mix lightly with fork to form soft, shaggy mass, adding up to 2 tablespoons more buttermilk or orange juice if necessary.

Turn out on lightly floured work surface and knead very gently to make soft dough. Pat or shape dough into 10-inch circle. Cut in quarters, then cut each quarter in thirds, making 12 wedges.

Place scones on baking sheet lined with parchment paper. Brush tops with cream and sprinkle with sugar. Bake at 425 degrees until golden, about 12 to 15 minutes.

This recipe yields 12 to 16 scones.

Each of 16 scones: 237 calories; 195 mg sodium; 40 mg cholesterol; 10 grams fat; 34 grams carbohydrates; 3 grams protein; 0.24 gram fiber.

SOURDOUGH BUTTERMILK BISCUITS AND SCONES

1 servings
Source: Scone Greats

- 1 cup **sourdough start**
- 1 cup **buttermilk**
- 1 **flour, possible 4 cups**
- 1 **egg**
- 3 tablespoons **oil**
- 1 tablespoon **sugar,** (2 or 3 tb sugar)
- 1 teaspoon **salt**
- 2 teaspoons **baking powder**
- 1 teaspoon **soda,** (1 1/2 or 2 tsp. if start is real sour)

The night before, or three to four hours before you intend to prepare these, combine sourdough start, buttermilk and 1 cup of the flour in a large bowl.

Cover and let stand at room temperature. When ready to use, add egg and oil; stir well.

Combine sugar, salt, baking powder and soda; sprinkle over top of batter. Fold in then add as much of the remaining flour to make a dough you can still stir (2 to 3 cups should do it).

To make Scones, dump batter out on a heavily floured board; sprinkle flour over top and roll out. Cut out scones.

Allow scones to rise a few minutes then fry on both sides in hot oil until golden brown.

Scone Greats

For Biscuits, add enough flour to make moderately stiff, so you can knead dough. Knead a few minutes then roll and cut out biscuits.

Drop both sides in oil or melted butter and place on cookie sheet.

Let rise for an hour then bake at 375°F for 25 minutes.

STRAWBERRY-PECAN SCONES

12 servings
Source: Scone Greats

2 cups **all-purpose flour**

¼ cup **sugar**

2 teaspoons **baking powder**

½ teaspoon **baking soda**

¼ teaspoon **salt**

3 tablespoons **margarine chilled and cut into small pieces**

8 ounces **vanilla low-fat yogurt**

Vegetable cooking spray

¼ cup **strawberry or raspberry spread, no-sugar-added**

2 tablespoons **finely chopped pecans**

Combine first 5 ingredients in a bowl; cut in margarine with a pastry blender until mixture resembles coarse meal. Add yogurt to dry ingredients, stirring just until dry ingredients are moistened. (Dough will be sticky.)

Turn dough out onto a lightly floured surface; with floured hands, knead 4 to 5 times. Pat dough into an 8-inch circle on a baking sheet coated with cooking spray. Cut dough into 12 wedges, cutting to but not through dough; make a small slit in center of each wedge. Place 1 teaspoon strawberry spread on top of each slit; sprinkle with pecans. Bake at 400 deg for 13 minutes or until golden. Yield: 1 dozen (serving size: 1 scone).

SWISS SCONES

12 servings
Source: Scone Greats

1 ½ cups **all-purpose flour**

¼ cup **sugar**

¼ teaspoon **baking soda**

1 ¼ teaspoons **baking powder**

¼ teaspoon **salt**

⅓ cup **cold butter, cut in small pieces**

½ cup **golden raisins**

grated rind of small orange

½ cup **buttermilk, (or 1/2 cup milk with 1 tablespoon lemon juice)**

enough milk or cream

to brush top of scones

2 tablespoons **sugar mixed with 1/4**

teaspoon ground cinnamon

Preheat oven to 425°F.

Place first 5 ingredients in a medium bowl and mix well. Cut butter into flour mixture with pastry cutter, until it resembles course meal. Add raisins and orange rind. Add buttermilk and mix with fork until dough leaves sides of bowl.

Place dough on floured board and pat into a circle or rectangle 1/2" thick. Cut in 2" circles or hearts with cookie cutter and place on lightly greased cookie sheet (parchment paper also works).

Space about 1 1/2" apart. Brush tops with cream or milk and sprinkle with sugar/cinnamon mixture (avoid getting sugar on cookie sheet as it will burn).

Bake for 10 minutes, until tops are lightly brown. Serve fresh from the oven or let cool and place in an airtight container.

Scones can be stored 1 – 2 days, but are best fresh.

Variations: Substitute dates for raisins or try chocolate chips.

Makes 12 scones.

TART CHERRY-&-VANILLA SCONES

8 servings
Source: Scone Greats

- ¾ cup **dried tart cherries**
- ¼ cup **boiling water**
- 1 ¾ cups **all-purpose flour**
- ⅓ cup **sugar**
- ¼ cup **yellow cornmeal**
- 2 teaspoons **baking powder**
- ¼ teaspoon **salt**
- 2 tablespoons **chilled stick margarine, cut in small pieces**
- 2 tablespoons **vegetable shortening**
- ⅓ cup **plain nonfat yogurt**
- ¼ cup **evaporated skimmed milk**
- 1 teaspoon **vanilla extract**
- ¼ teaspoon **butter extract**
- **Vegetable cooking spray**
- 1 **egg white, lightly beaten**
- 2 teaspoons **sugar**

Combine cherries and boiling water in a bowl; cover and let stand 10 minutes or until softened. Drain and set aside. Combine flour, 1/3 cup sugar, cornmeal, baking powder, and salt in a large bowl; cut in the margarine and shortening with a pastry blender or 2 knives until mixture resembles coarse meal.

Combine cherries, yogurt, milk, and extracts, and add to dry ingredients, stirring just until dry ingredients are moistened (dough will be sticky). Pat the dough with floured hands into an 8-inch round cake pan coated with cooking spray.

Brush egg white over surface of dough, and sprinkle with 2 teaspoons sugar. Bake at 425°F for 20 minutes or until a wooden pick inserted in center comes out clean.

TEA SCONES

8 servings
Source: Scone Greats

----basic tea scones-----

1 cup **Flour**

1 teaspoon **Baking powder**

¼ teaspoon **Salt**

1 tablespoon **Sugar replacement**

¼ cup **Margarine, cold**

1 **Egg**

¼ cup **Evaporated milk, freeze the rest**

Sift flour, baking powder, salt and sugar replacement. Cut in cold margarine as for pie crust. Beat egg and evaporated milk together thoroughly; into flour mixture. Knead gently on lightly floured board.

Divide the dough in half; roll each half into a circles. Cut the into quarters. Place on lightly greased cookie sheet. Brush tops with milk. Bake at 450f for 15 minutes or until done.

TEATIME SCONES

10 servings
Source: Scone Greats

2 cups **Flour, all purpose**

1 tablespoon **Sugar**

½ teaspoon **Baking Powder**

½ teaspoon **Baking Soda**

¼ teaspoon **Salt**

⅓ cup **Butter, chilled**

1 **Egg**

½ cup **Buttermilk**

1 teaspoon **Vanilla**

Scone Greats

In large bowl, combine flour, sugar, baking powder, baking soda and salt. With a pastry blender or two knives cut in butter until mixture resembles coarse crumbs. In separate bowl, combine egg, buttermilk and vanilla. Using fork, stir into dry ingredients to form a soft dough. Gather into ball.

Turn out onto lightly floured surface; knead lightly 10 times. With lightly floured hands, dough in 1/2 in thick round. Using 2 1/2 in. cookie cutter, cut dough into rounds, gathering scraps together until dough is all used up. Place rounds on lightly greased baking sheet. Bake in 425°F (220°C) oven 12 to 15 minutes or until golden brown and risen. Let cool on wire racks. Serve warm.

YOGURT CHEDDAR SCONES

15 servings
Source: Scone Greats

1 ¾ cups **all-purpose flour**

1 tablespoon **granulated sugar**

1 tablespoon **baking powder**

1 teaspoon **baking soda**

¾ teaspoons **salt**

¼ cup **butter, cold**

¾ cups **cheddar cheese, shred**

1 cup **1% plain yogurt**

In large bowl, mix together flour, sugar, baking powder, baking soda and salt; cut in butter until mixture resembles coarse crumbs. Stir in cheese. Add yogurt all at once; stir with fork to make soft, slightly sticky dough. On lightly floured surface, knead dough gently 6 times or until smooth. Gently pat out dough to 1-inch thick round.

Using 2-inch round cutter, cut out rounds. Gather up scraps and pat out dough once morel; cut into rounds.

Bake on ungreased baking sheet at 425°F 220°C for 12 to 15 minutes or until puffed and golden. Transfer to racks and let cool.

Chapter 2: N–Z

Index

, 16, 16, 16
(1 large apple), 4
(1 stick) chilled, 29
(1 stick) cold unsalted, 25, 58
(1/2 cup) butter, 32
(1/2 stick) chilled, 37
(3oz) finely shredded, 19
(60 g) butter, 56
(about 3/4 cup) dried, 32
(apricots, 32
(optional), 25
country cream, 24
lemon curd, 24
+ 3 t flour, 33
-----, 71
----basic tea scones-----, 77
--apple pear butter:---, 53
--for the scones:---, 16
--for the topping:---, 16
--fruits:---, 16
--scones---, 32
--topping---, 4
--topping:---, 51
-salt, 9, 18, 40
-water, 9
1% plain yogurt, 78
2 cup butter or margarine, 36
2 cup buttermilk, 36
2 teaspoon grated orange peel, 36
4 cup dried currants, 36
4 teaspoon salt, 36
= (1/2 pepper from a jar, 61
= (jiffy recommended), 60

= (old bay recommended), 61
= (tabasco recommended), 61
=== salad ===, 61
a couple pinches salt, 60
a few drops hot sauce, 61
additional, 58
additional sugar, 2
all purpose flour, 3, 9
all-purpose flour, 2, 4, 5, 6, 8, 12, 14, 16, 18, 19, 20, 23, 25, 26, 27, 29, 31, 32, 32, 34, 36, 37, 38, 44, 46, 50, 51, 53, 54, 59, 74, 75, 76, 78
all-purpose seasoning, 61
almonds, 49
and granulated sugar, 32
apple juice, 53
apple; chopped, 8
apples, 3, 7
apricots, 8
at room temperature, 49
baby spinach leaves – (abt 1/4 lb), 61
baking powder, 1, 2, 3, 3, 4, 5, 6, 7, 8, 9, 10, 12, 13, 14, 15, 16, 18, 18, 19, 20, 21, 22, 23, 25, 26, 27, 28, 29, 30, 31, 32, 32, 33, 36, 38, 38, 40, 44, 46, 48, 49, 50, 51, 54, 55, 56, 57, 58, 59, 63, 63, 65, 65, 67, 68, 69, 70, 72, 73, 74, 75, 76, 77, 77, 78
baking soda, 2, 3, 4, 10, 15, 16, 20, 23, 25, 27, 27, 35, 37, 39, 41, 43, 50, 54, 58, 59, 72, 74, 75, 77, 78
baskets strawberries, 21
basking soda, 18

Index

beat together:, 64, 67
beaten egg yolk, 39
bicarbonate of soda, 34
bisquick, 8, 62
bittersweet, 22
boiling water, 76
box biscuit mix, 60
bran flakes cereal, 6
brandy, 36
bread flour, 34
brown sugar, 8, 14, 38, 51, 63, 64, 67, 67
buckwheat flour, 14
bulk hot sausage, 62
butter, 1, 2, 5, 6, 9, 11, 14, 15, 19, 19, 22, 24, 25, 28, 30, 39, 41, 47, 47, 49, 55, 57, 58, 59, 63, 64, 66, 67, 77, 78
butter extract, 76
butter or margarine, 4, 31, 38, 44, 45, 51, 56, 69, 70
butter or margarine;, 21
buttermilk, 2, 11, 15, 16, 24, 35, 41, 51, 73, 75, 77
buttermilk (180ml), 57
buttermilk or orange juice, 72
buttermilk or plain yogurt, 58
buttermilk;, 49
cake flour, 32, 59, 65, 68, 72
canned biscuits, 42
cans salmon with bones – (14 oz ea), 61
cayenne pepper, 63
cheddar cheese, 78
chilled and cut into small pieces, 74
chilled butter, 33
chilled stick margarine, 27, 27, 50, 76
chips (6 oz), 21
chocolate,, 22
chopped candied ginger, 2
chopped crystallized ginger, 29
chopped dried fruit, 32
chopped flat-leaf parsley, 61
chopped green pepper, 41
chopped onion, 41
chopped parsley, 42
chopped pecans, 48
chopped pitted dates, 50
chopped roasted red pepper – (to 4), 61
chopped), 61
cinnamon, 7, 64, 67
clove garlic, 42
coarse sugar (optional), 39
cold, 11
cold apple juice or water, 7
cold butter, 24, 75
cold butter or margarine,, 19
cold unsalted butter, 12, 16
corn syrup, 13
cranberries, 54
cream, 60, 72
cream (or half-and-half), 32
cream of tartar, 37, 41, 43
currants, 15, 30, 35, 49, 59, 66, 66, 68, 69, 70
cut in small pieces, 19
cut into small pieces, 27, 27, 50
dash cinnamon, 28
dash salt, 28, 35
devonshire cream and preserves, 66
dice, 25
diced dried pears, 2
diced or small plump dried, 16
double-acting baking powder, 66
dried apples, 3, 51, 53
dried cherries, 20
dried dill, 42
dried herbs, 43
dried oregano, 19
dried pears, 53
dried sour cherries, 72
dried sweet cherries, 11
dried tart cherries, 33, 76
dry mustard, 18

Scone Greats

egg, 2, 8, 22, 27, 29, 33, 35, 40, 42, 49, 51, 53, 59, 69, 70, 72, 73, 77, 77
egg white, 20, 20, 64, 67, 76
egg whites, 3, 50, 61
egg yolk, 35, 47, 64, 66, 67
egg yolks, 24
eggs, 1, 21, 24, 30, 38, 45, 47, 48, 55, 56, 63, 64, 67, 68
endive, 61
enough milk or cream, 75
evaporated milk, 77
evaporated skimmed milk, 76
extra sugar, 24
extra-virgin olive oil - (to 1/3), 61
figs, 16
fine sea salt, 25
finely chopped dried, 8
finely chopped onion, 19
finely chopped pecans, 74
finely-chopped rosemary - (4 small stems), 60
finely-grated orange zest, 72
firmly packed brown sugar, 50
flour, 1, 7, 15, 18, 21, 22, 38, 41, 42, 42, 43, 49, 56, 58, 63, 66, 73, 77, 77
flour;all purpose*, 40
for brushing, 16
fresh lemon juice, 24, 47
fresh yeast, 34
freshly-ground black pepper, 61, 61
frozen cranberries, 27
fruit cocktail in juice, 38
g zest of one large orange, 57
ginger, 8
golden raisins, 27, 32, 46, 75
granola, 14, 38
granulated sugar, 5, 8, 20, 31, 32, 38, 51, 54, 69, 70, 78
grated cheddar cheese, 43, 63
grated lemon zest, 12
grated orange or lemon zest, 16
grated orange peel, 31, 57
grated orange rind, 27
grated orange rind (orange, 15
grated parmesan cheese, 19
grated rind of small orange, 75
grated zest of 1 lemon or orange, 68
grated zest of one lemon, 48
ground allspice, 53
ground cinnamon, 3, 4, 4, 5, 6, 6, 39, 50, 51, 51, 53, 54
ground cloves, 53
ground cumin, 57
ground ginger, 2, 38, 51
ground nutmeg, 3, 4, 51, 58
half and half, 53
hamburger, 42
head frissee lettuce, 61
heavy (whipping) cream, 8
heavy cream, 12, 29, 33, 48, 55
heavy whipping cream, 28
honey, 1, 4, 4, 47, 54, 54
into pieces, 37, 65
italian bread crumbs, 61
jam or jelly, 16
kosher salt, 10
large egg, 24, 32, 66
large eggs, 12, 31, 44
lemon extract, 48, 49
lemon juice, 57
lemon peel, 46, 47, 49
lemon zest, 24, 24
lemons, 48
lg egg, 6, 8, 14
lg egg white, 5
lg eggs, 19
lg red apple, 6
lg tart apples, 4
light, 32
light brown sugar, 6, 53
low-fat buttermilk, 27
lowfat 1% milk, 5
lowfat 2% milk, 3
margarine, 3, 3, 54, 74, 77
marjoram, 42
mealy potatoes, 42

Index

medium lemons, 45
medium limes, 45
medium-grind yellow cornmeal, 11
melted butter, 48
milk, 4, 6, 8, 8, 14, 18, 19, 21, 22, 25, 30, 31, 32, 33, 37, 39, 40, 43, 56, 63, 66, 69, 70
milk (about), 19
minced orange zest, 59
mini chocolate chips, 31
mix together:, 64, 67
molasses, 39
natural applesauce, 54
navel orange, 61
nutmeg, 24
oil, 18, 42, 73
oil for frying, 42
or honey crunch, 3
orange juice, 59
orange or lemon rind;grated, 33
orange zest, 24, 60, 61
package semisweet chocolate, 21
parmesan cheese, 63
part, 15
pastry flour, 28, 65
peanut butter, 22
peanuts, 22
peeled apple, 54
pepper, 42
pieces deli-sliced glazed smoked ham – (abt 2 oz), 60
plain nonfat yogurt, 27, 76
plus 1 tablespoon sugar, 28
plus 2 tablespoons sugar, 11
pn salt, 18
potato or soy milk, 13
powdered sage, 42
raisins, 1, 3, 7, 9, 28, 58, 65
raisins (120g), 57
raisins or currants, 18
raisins or dried fruit (optional), 64, 67
raisins/ a pricots/, 16
raspberry jam, 44
raspberry preserves, 57
recipe nutmeg whipped cream, 39
red wine vinegar, 61
rinsed fresh blueberries, 12
rolled oats, 9, 53, 54
romaine heart, 61
room temp., 21
rosemary and ham scones, 61
saffron threads, 57
salt, 1, 2, 3, 4, 5, 6, 7, 8, 12, 15, 16, 19, 21, 22, 24, 27, 27, 29, 31, 32, 32, 34, 37, 38, 39, 41, 42, 42, 43, 44, 46, 48, 49, 50, 51, 53, 54, 55, 56, 56, 57, 59, 59, 61, 61, 63, 63, 66, 66, 67, 68, 72, 73, 74, 75, 76, 77, 77, 78
salted butter, 65
savory, 42
see below, 16
self-raising flour, 56
self-rising flour, 35
serving (optional), 25
sharp cheddar cheese, 19, 62
shortening, 7
shortening or lard, 40
shredded cheddar cheese, 5
sifted cake flour, 27
skim milk, 4, 54
skim milk or 1 beaten, 20
slightly beaten egg white, 39
slivered almonds, 2
sm rome apple, 5
small pieces, 29
small red onion, 61
soda, 73
sour cream, 18, 24, 28
sourdough start, 73
soy margarine, 13
stemmed and sliced, 21
strawberry or raspberry spread, 74
sugar, 1, 2, 4, 4, 7, 8, 9, 12, 15, 16, 16, 18, 21, 22, 23, 24, 24, 26, 27, 27, 29, 30, 32, 33, 34, 35, 36, 37, 41, 44, 45, 46, 47, 47, 48, 48, 49, 55, 55, 56,

Scone Greats

56, 57, 58, 59, 60, 65, 66, 66, 68, 68, 72, 73, 74, 75, 76, 76, 77
sugar for sprinkling, 58
sugar mixed with 1/4, 75
sugar replacement, 77
sugar;granulated, 40
tabasco pepper sauce, 19
tart cherries, 32
teaspoon ground cinnamon, 75
to brush top of scones, 75
toasted coarsely broken, 8
toasted wheat germ, 5
topping, 4
topping - mix together:, 64, 67
unbleached all-purpose flour, 10, 30
unbleached flour, 72
unbleached white flour, 48
unprocessed wheat bran, 50
unsalted butter, 8, 16, 29, 35, 37, 43, 53, 53
unsifted all purpose flour, 55
unsweetened applesauce, 20, 20, 51
up to 6 tablespoons), 69, 70
vanilla, 64, 67, 77
vanilla extract, 8, 14, 22, 24, 69, 70, 72, 76
vanilla low-fat yogurt, 50, 74
vegetable cooking spray, 27, 27, 50, 74, 76

vegetable oil, 6, 34, 42, 61
vegetable shortening, 35, 66, 76
very cold butter, 68, 72
walnuts**, 8
warm milk and water, 34
warm water, 34
warmed maple syrup for, 25
water, 42, 48, 64, 67
water to 4 as needed, 46
wheat bran, 13
wheat germ, 3, 4, 4, 4
wheat germ original, 3
whipped butter for serving, 25
whipping cream, 21, 24, 44, 46, 56, 59, 65, 66, 68, 68
white chocolate, 8
white chocolate chips, 31
white flour, 63, 67, 69, 70
white of a large egg, 58
whole milk, 1
whole wheat flour, 3, 9, 20
whole wheat flour (260g), 57
whole wheat pastry flour, 13
whole-wheat flour, 19, 50
wholemeal flour, 13
worcestershire sauce, 42
yellow cornmeal, 26, 76
yogurt or cream, 64, 67
yolk of a large egg, 58

Made in the USA
Lexington, KY
25 March 2014